THE AGILE INVESTOR

Also by Stephen Leeb

Market Timing for the Nineties

THE Agile Investor

PROFITING FROM THE END OF BUY AND HOLD

Stephen Leeb

and Roger Conrad

HarperBusiness
A Division of HarperCollins*Publishers*

HarperCollins books may be purchased for educational, business, or sales promotional use. For information please write: Special Markets Department, HarperCollins Publishers, Inc., 10 East 53rd Street, New York, NY 10022.

FIRST EDITION

Designed by Alma Hochhauser Orenstein

Library of Congress Cataloging-in-Publication Data

Leeb, Stephen, 1946–
    The agile investor : profiting from the end of buy and hold / Stephen Leeb and Roger Conrad. — 1st ed.
      p. cm.
    Includes index.
    ISBN 0-88730-760-4
    1. Investments—United States.   2. Inflation (Finance).
I. Conrad, Roger. II. Title.
HG4910.L448   1997
332.6'0973—dc20   96-33128

97 98 99 00 01 ❖/RRD 10 9 8 7 6 5 4

CONTENTS

To Donna, Timmy, Willie, Sarah and Nate

ACKNOWLEDGMENTS

We would first like to thank my wife, Donna, for her help in all phases of the project. Thanks to the staff of *Personal Finance* for their help in the formation of ideas, especially Greg Dorsey, Gregg Early, Scott Ireland, Debra Piazzi and Trae Underwood, who aided in the design of many of the charts and graphs. Deep appreciation is also in order for my long-time friend Frank Mlynarczyk, for his insights and daily consultation.

To *Personal Finance*'s publisher Walter Pearce and marketing director Vicki Moffit, we offer our gratitude for their support and encouragement for this project. And a special round of thanks to our agent, Al Zuckerman, and editor Cynthia Barrett at Harper-Collins.

INTRODUCTION

Facing the Coming Inflation

This book is about forecasts. So let me start by making a few.

Sometime in the next ten years, inflation will crest at over 20 percent. Mortgage interest rates will hit the high teens. A gallon of low-grade gasoline will sell for $5. The value of an ounce of gold will reach $1,000 and the price of a single family home will double.

The stock market will finish the next ten years about where it is today, well behind inflation. But in between, we'll have to suffer through at least one crushing bear market, during which the average stock will drop 50 percent or more. There's also the possibility of a crushing depression, which could force millions out of work and generally bankrupt the country.

Believe it or not, I'm an optimist by nature. During my twenty-plus years on Wall Street, I've more than once been dubbed a "perpetual bull." I was bullish back in late 1990, when Iraq's Saddam Hussein was threatening to cut off the world's oil supplies. I was a buyer of stocks in the aftermath of the October 1987 1,000-point stock market crash, when most analysts and investors were running for the hills.

I was also a strong bull back in the early 1980s, when the Great Bull Market of the 1980s and '90s was in its infancy. Then I wrote a book—*Getting in on the Ground Floor*—in which I predicted that the Dow Jones Industrial Average would reach above 4000 by the early

1990s. Back then the Dow was at 1000 and I was pronounced nuts. Today it's heading toward 6000.

What's convinced me that dark times lie ahead? Higher inflation. Thousands of things can affect the stock market's daily fluctuations. But over the long haul, market forecasting basically boils down to inflation forecasting. Simply, if inflation is under control, stocks do well. If it's raging, stocks do poorly.

In 1984, 1987 and again in 1990, the big economic forces pointed toward low inflation. Here in the latter 1990s, the tables have turned. Instead, what we're headed for will look more like the 1970s, when high inflation caused a series of booms and busts for the economy and the stock market.

One final forecast: There will be staggering opportunities to get rich over the next ten years—even more than there were during the Great Bull Market of the 1980s and early 1990s. But these opportunities will be different. Whereas financial assets like stocks and bonds ruled the '80s, "real" assets like energy, gold and real estate will reign supreme as the investments of choice in the decade ahead.

I fully realize that what I've just said flies in the face of everything you've heard in the media and on Wall Street recently. After fifteen-plus years of watching stocks go up, who can blame journalists, brokers, media personalities or anyone else for assuming the good times will last forever?

In today's America, people are taught to rely on "experts," rather than think for themselves. And what's the word from the investment gurus like Louis Rukeyser and Peter Lynch, who have attained an almost godlike stature? Simply that inflation is no real threat, that stocks will rise forever and that "buy and hold" is a sure-fire road to riches.

Back in the early 1980s, most big-name advisors and investors were just as deeply convinced that inflation would forever be out of control, and that stocks and bonds should be avoided. Wall Street has a notoriously short memory. One reason is that a good percentage of today's mutual fund managers, stock analysts and investment counsellors were in grade school when the current bull market began. Most of us who were around are too busy trying to make money day-to-day to notice when the economy and the markets make a sea change.

The rocky, high-inflation 1970s gave way to the low-inflation, steady growth 1980s. So will the current era fade into an era of rapid inflation and jagged economic growth. Those who don't change with the times will get crushed under their wheels.

The Three Building Blocks

Part 1 of this book spotlights the three building blocks of the coming inflation. The first is a growing cry throughout the world for faster economic growth, brought on by a twenty-year decline in the average person's buying power and our inability to reverse that trend through improved productivity and education. The second building block is the dawn of a new bull market in the essential commodities that power all industries. The third is the huge debt level in the world economy, which will force governments to either inflate or face chaos.

Part 2 of the book pinpoints the investments historically proven to prosper in times of higher inflation and those you should shun. The latter 1990s promise massive new growth opportunities in the energy industry, and producers of basic commodities will thrive. Real estate will prosper. And, just as the 1980s were punctuated by down markets, so the decade ahead will have its share of bull market runs for stocks and bonds. In fact, judging from the 1970s, the market upmoves of the latter 1990s should be even more rewarding than those of the '80s!

The difference is that financial markets in the latter 1990s are going to be much more volatile. Timing will be more essential than ever to success. Hard assets like real estate and gold will trade places with financial assets as the long-term portfolio picks of choice. It will still be an age of opportunity—but the opportunities will be considerably different from those of the 1980s. For stocks, buy and hold is out; buying and selling at precisely the right moment is in.

Our goal in writing this book is to point the way toward negotiating these trickier opportunities. Change is inevitable. This book will help to make it your friend, not your enemy.

Inflation's Three Building Blocks

The Cry for Growth

"Throw the bums out!" has been the voters' battle cry in almost every major world election during the 1990s. From Ottawa to Athens, incumbent politicians of all stripes have become an endangered species.

What's behind voters' discontent? A plea for faster economic growth, more and better jobs and fatter paychecks. This cry for growth is the first and most important building block of the coming inflation.

For the better part of two decades, the world's governments have been fixated on fighting inflation, often at the expense of promoting economic growth. That's boosted corporate profits and helped the Dow Jones Industrial Average quintuple. The average worker, however, has actually lost ground. The voters' message to elected officials now is simply this: Either help us or find a new job.

Faced with that ultimatum, it's only a matter of time before governments shift the primary focus of economic policy from fighting inflation at all costs to boosting growth. Their shift will produce higher inflation—ultimately cresting at more than 20 percent—for the next ten to fifteen years.

Politicians on the Run

In the United States, the cry for growth was first heard loud and clear during the astounding 1992 presidential election. Arkansas Governor Bill Clinton came out of nowhere to defeat President George Bush, whose popularity had been over 70 percent just two years before.

Americans vote their pocketbooks. When the economy is doing well, presidents get reelected. When things go sour, as they did for Jimmy Carter in 1980, presidents get the boot.

The U.S. economy was steaming ahead in the months before the '92 election. The Gross Domestic Product (GDP) was growing at a robust 4.5 percent annual rate during the last quarter of 1992, with little or no inflation. The unemployment rate was falling, and most economists were upbeat about the future.

Nonetheless, a full 62 percent of the voters decided that things were bad enough to throw out the incumbent, an authentic war hero who had won the world's adulation for standing up to Iraqi strongman Saddam Hussein less than two years earlier. In his place, they cast a vote for either Clinton—the little-known governor of a small state—or quixotic billionaire Ross Perot.

In the past, Mr. Bush would have been guaranteed a landslide win, given the GDP's seemingly robust rate of growth, his achievements and his rivals' shortcomings. Instead, he got the smallest share of the vote for an incumbent president since William Howard Taft in 1912—even worse than Herbert Hoover did at the height of the Great Depression in 1932!

Bush lost because 4 or even 5 percent GDP growth just wasn't enough. Then as now, despite the assurances of "experts" that things were going well, millions of Americans were deeply dissatisfied with their economic present and worried about their economic future. It would have taken growth a lot faster than a noninflationary 4.5 percent to change that and save Mr. Bush.

Some Republicans might say otherwise. But the message of the just-as-astounding 1994 U.S. congressional elections was also a cry for faster growth. Voters threw out the Democratic majority that had endured for more than forty years, in the process discarding many once-popular congressmen. Again, despite assurances from economists that everything was just peachy, voters thought otherwise. They showed it by throwing out those who they thought were responsible—this time the Democrats.

Political upheaval has been even more earthshaking abroad. Incumbent politicians worldwide are suffering humiliating defeats, regardless of ideology. On the liberal side, the once-ruling French Socialists have been relegated to a small minority party in the space of a few years.

On the conservative side, Canada's formerly ruling Progressive Conservative Party, or Tories, suffered perhaps the worst defeat by a political party in modern history, losing an unprecedented 153 of their 155 seats in the October 1993 elections. That year, Greece returned its Socialists to power, despite an array of scandals. The widely discredited Polish Communists were voted back in by an electorate fed up with capitalist parties' inability to improve economic conditions.

Even the Japanese Liberal Democratic Party, which held that country in an iron grip for forty years, was reduced to a minority party. Italy brought the ex-Communists to power for the first time.

And the victors in these elections have had little time to celebrate. Recent voter polls around the world show that most will probably suffer even greater defeats when new elections are held.

Losing Ground

Why are people so dissatisfied with what on paper seems to be a healthy economy? Because the benefits of steady growth—the same formula that made everyone happy in bygone years—aren't trickling down to the average person.

Even the soaring stock market, which reflects the ballooning corporate profits, is almost solely a rich man's toy. According to data generated by economists James M. Poterba and Andrew A. Samick, 98 percent of the value of publicly traded stocks is in the hands of the wealthiest 20 percent of households, leaving just 2 percent for the remaining 80 percent.

Annual economic growth of 4.5 percent with no inflation is just dandy for corporate executives and investors who are watching their profits surge. The wrenching truth is that, for the first time in memory, the majority of Americans have stopped participating in the forward march of wealth.

Quite the contrary. Over the past twenty years Americans have seen their buying power drop. Unlike the Great Depression of the 1930s, the decline has not been sudden or steep. But it has been relentless. Worse still, it shows no sign of reversing, and it has begun to feed on itself.

Our graph labeled "Real Weekly Earnings" shows average weekly wages, adjusted for inflation, since the early 1900s. This is a pretty good approximation of what the average person has been able to buy year-in, year-out.

Throughout most of this century, Americans' inflation-adjusted, or "real," wages rose. The rich got richer, but everyone else did too. That trend halted about 1972 and has been in full reverse ever since.

Until the late 1980s, there was a loophole of sorts to the problem of falling incomes—the growing number of two-income families, which helped pick up some of the slack of diminished paychecks. From the 1960s on, increasing numbers of married and unmarried women entered the workforce. Consequently, when real wages began falling in the 1970s, American families with two incomes could still aspire to get ahead, as the loss in buying power of a single paycheck was camouflaged to some extent by the addition of a second salary.

By 1988, however, having two incomes was no longer a matter of choice for most families, but a necessity. Worse, the tragedy of the 1990s is that, for many, even two incomes have become heartbreakingly insufficient.

Take a look at our second graph, "Real Weekly Family Earnings." This shows the median income for families in the United States since 1982, adjusted for inflation. Since 1990, real median family income has dropped by 2.4 percent, and is still falling. This grim reality—falling family incomes—probably more than anything else is fueling Americans' growing anger and frustration.

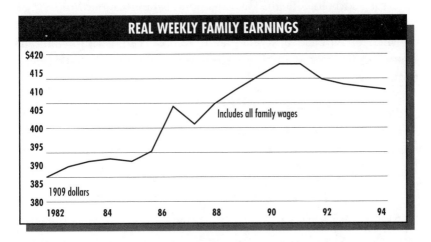

REAL WEEKLY FAMILY EARNINGS

Includes all family wages

1909 dollars

The only remaining alternative for many families to boost incomes is to send the kids to work. A few years ago, this would have sounded like a throwaway line, a joke. Some joke. Look at the August 1994 headline from the *New York Times*. As it shows, three-income families are becoming a well-entrenched trend.

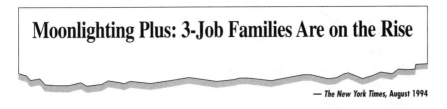

Moonlighting Plus: 3-Job Families Are on the Rise

— *The New York Times*, August 1994

At the turn of this century, it was common for families to put their children to work, and relatively rare for anyone to be sent off to get a college education. Since President Franklin D. Roosevelt's New Deal in the 1930s, the reverse has been true. But as the evidence of falling real incomes shows, we may be heading back to those dark days again.

Conditions today are better than they were in the 1930s and even the 1950s by most measures. But that's not the point. The direction of one's standard of living—whether or not things are getting better—is what counts, not the absolute level of wealth.

Workers on the bottom rungs of the income ladder may now own a TV, a VCR, a compact disc player and a reasonably new car. But it's getting harder every year for them to put food on the table, let alone send their kids to college. The direction of their standard of living is down and they are not going to accept the situation passively.

Michael Novick, a scholar at the conservative think tank the American Enterprise Institute, summed up the import of this beautifully in a *Wall Street Journal* article.

People do not love democracy if it does not bring improvement in their economic conditions. They will not be satisfied with democracy if all it means is the opportunity to vote every two years. Typically, they do not ask for utopia but would like to see the possibility of solid economic progress for their families over the next three to four years.

There is hard data to support this point. Real incomes today are more than twice what they were in 1957. Yet as David Myers points out in his book *Pursuit of Happiness,* a much smaller portion of individuals say they are very happy today compared with 1957. It's where you're going, not where you've been. And as long as that direction is down for the majority, there is going to be a cry for faster growth.

Two Americas

Not all Americans' incomes have dropped since the 1970s. The U.S. economy has kept growing. But only the rich have been getting richer; the rest have been falling further and further behind.

Rising inequalities mean the economy will have to grow that much faster in order for the benefits to trickle down to the less fortunate. That's why President Bush was beaten in 1992 and the Democratic Congress was whipped in 1994. The benefits of the relatively rapid growth were being reaped by Wall Street and corporate executives, not rank and file workers.

Pro-growth Republicans like Jack Kemp and publisher Steve Forbes argue that society as a whole cannot and should not target an exact level of wealth distribution as optimal. Rather, they suggest that government should merely promote opportunity for all to get ahead.

Unfortunately, inequalities and falling incomes feed on each other. When wealth distribution gets too far out of whack, opportunities for those at the bottom to catch up or even keep pace become increasingly scarce.

Fewer opportunities mean that fewer people will succeed in lifting themselves up. This increases wealth inequality, which diminishes opportunity further and so on. Government guarantee or no, the more extreme the cycle gets, the harder it is for anyone to do anything to reverse it.

A case in point is the educational system: the modern world's now rapidly closing window of opportunity, the subject of chapter 3. In an increasingly technical and interconnected world, a college education is more critical than ever to getting ahead. Unfortunately, the soaring price of attending even public universities has put this vital credential out of reach for many.

How great is the country's growing economic "Grand Canyon"? Consider these three mind-boggling comparisons, produced by the Tax Foundation.

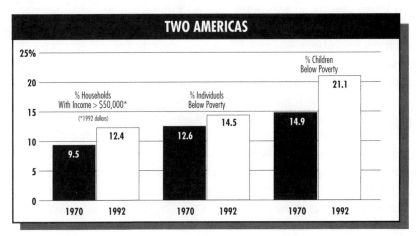

The first shows the percentage of households with incomes above $50,000—affluent Americans—in 1992 compared with the percentage in 1970, adjusted for inflation. As you can see, the number of relatively affluent Americans has grown over the last twenty years.

The second and third comparisons tell a different story. For starters, the percentage of individuals below the poverty line rose from 12.6 percent in 1970 to 14.5 percent in 1992. More alarmingly, the percentage of children living below the poverty line increased from 14.9 percent to a whopping 21.1 percent.

Higher crime rates, a lack of skilled workers to fuel productivity gains and economic growth and a dearth of markets for industry's products are three consequences of the economic Grand Canyon. The violence that gripped France in 1789, Russia in 1914, China in the early 1900s and this country at the turn of the century is stark evidence of what happens to societies that let huge inequalities go too long unchecked.

The Inflation "Cure"

Motivated by fear of landslide losses, America's politicians will go to great lengths to avoid letting things slide that far. But their only choice will be to pump up economic growth in hopes that both rich and poor will benefit. And as long as inequalities are rising and real incomes continue to decline for the large majority, their task will be that much harder.

There are two ways for governments to energize economic growth: fiscal policy (government spending) and monetary policy (control of money-supply growth with interest rates). Beginning with the recession of the early 1990s, the world's central banks have increasingly stoked money-supply growth to fire up overall growth.

Here in America it may take some time for fiscal policies to become as inflationary as monetary policies have been. Fear of government deficits and the ideology that balanced budgets will be a panacea for our problems have thus far stymied most new pro-growth policies. But it's only a matter of time before this changes.

Approaches will differ. Republicans as a group favor tax cuts, while Democrats generally place more reliance on targeted spending increases. Whichever road to stimulus they choose, the result will be the same: a revved-up economy.

Ultimately, this will prove to be an ineffective answer to the problems of falling incomes and growing inequalities. But it will ease the pain, and in the short time horizon of the politician, that's what's important.

Inflation is the inevitable consequence of stimulating an already growing economy such as we have in the mid-1990s. The table "More Growth = More Inflation" compares rates of growth—as measured by the twelve-month change in the Commerce Department's Index of Coincident Indicators—with consumer and commodity price inflation since 1955.

MORE GROWTH = MORE INFLATION				
Change in Coincident Economic Indicators vs. CPI and ACPPI				
Years	Avg 12-Mo. Change Coincident Indicators	Years	Average CPI	Average ACPPI
1955–63, 1979–93	2.22%	1955–63, 1979–93	1.96%	0.71%
1964–78	3.51	1964–78	6.66	7.17
Assumes growth precedes inflation by 2 years.				

The table shows that there have been two periods of basically low inflation: 1955–1963 and 1979–1993. Over that time, the Consumer Price Index (CPI) rose an average of 1.96 percent a year while the All-Commodity Producer Price Index (ACPPI) rose 0.71 percent. Low inflation was accompanied by modest annual economic growth of 2.22 percent.

From 1964 through 1978, the economy revved up considerably to a 3.51 percent rate of growth. Faster growth, however, came at the heavy price of faster inflation. The CPI averaged a whopping 6.66 percent annual rate while the ACPPI averaged 7.17 percent.

Growth and inflation don't mirror each other exactly month-to-month, or even year-to-year. But as the table shows, they do have a close long-term relationship. Financial markets today are very attuned to the latest twists and turns in the economy. When growth has been perceived to be too fast and potentially inflationary, interest rates have risen and stocks and bonds have fallen.

Apart from Wall Street, however, the generally low level of inflation over the past decade or so has created a profound complacency. Most economists, politicians, businesspeople and journalists simply believe "it can't happen here." The years of double-digit price increases during the 1970s have been forgotten.

Today, it seems, only a lunatic would say that the next crisis confronting America will be severe inflation, causing at least as much economic stress as the Great Depression of the 1930s. But that's where we're headed.

As real incomes drop and economic inequalities increase, Americans' cry for faster growth and more pay will grow ever more shrill. To save their skins, politicians will try to do the only thing they can: pump up economic growth. That means more inflation.

2

Made in America

"Give me your tired, your poor, your huddled masses yearning to breathe free!" From El Salvador to Indonesia, the world's teeming billions still hearken to the Statue of Liberty's message that America is a land of opportunity. Here, she sings, hard work and a little luck can earn anyone a good life: fat paychecks, fast cars, a family, a house in the suburbs, luxurious vacations, the best in consumer products and a comfortable retirement.

America's age-old promise never rang more truly than during the two decades following World War II. After saving the world for democracy, this country entered a period of sustained prosperity the likes of which have never been equaled. The rich got richer and everyone else got rich ever faster. The more education a person had, the better he or she did. But even a high school diploma was usually a ticket to success. The economy grew swiftly, and with virtually no inflation.

The key to America's unprecedented prosperity following World War II was rising productivity. For over two decades, a combination of technological advance, expanding international trade and investment enabled workers in scores of industries to produce more products more efficiently. Workers were rewarded with rising salaries. Consumers chose from an ever-increasing variety of products. Living standards rose steadily and dramatically.

Today, America's productivity is still rising. Unfortunately, it no longer benefits most workers. In fact, productivity gains are typically used by companies to trim labor costs, making workers expendable and considerably less empowered to ask for wage hikes.

Rising productivity's downward pressure on workers' wages is a major reason for the two-decade decline in real incomes and rise in inequalities. Until rising productivity once again generates real wealth, it will be a major force behind the cry for faster economic growth.

Competing with the World

The dramatic boost in American manufacturing productivity over the past decade is often held up as one of the world's great economic success stories. Industries from autos to steel were frequently derided in the 1970s and '80s as dinosaurs, with inefficient management and bloated workforces that were simply incapable of competing with the "more efficient" Japanese and other emerging nations. Doomsayers painted a bleak picture in which the country would have no industry of its own.

Nothing has proven to be further from the truth. In fact, spurred by the brutal foreign competition of the 1970s and early 1980s, American industry is widely considered to be the most competitive in the world. U.S. manufacturers have become more efficient every year.

One great example: the American "mini-mill" steel industry. These superefficient high-tech outfits continue to win world market share from developing world competitors, despite the much higher wages they must pay workers.

Unfortunately, unlike during the 1950s and '60s, today's gains in manufacturing productivity are not being used to produce more goods with the same inputs. Instead, they're enabling companies to produce the same amount of goods with fewer inputs, thereby keeping their costs low enough to compete abroad.

That's why the productivity gains of the 1990s are not translating into higher incomes and living standards for workers. They boost corporate profits but increase inequalities and social tensions.

Take a look at the graphs, which compare the average weekly

wages of manufacturing workers—adjusted for inflation—to manufacturing productivity from 1960 to 1994. Up until about 1978, the
more workers produced the more money they made. After that, the
pattern began to change dramatically. The line measuring productivity in manufacturing continued upwards, accelerating in the latter years of the 1980s and early 1990s. At the same time, average
real weekly wages actually lost ground.

Free trade and the globalization of the world economy have
changed the nature of manufacturing productivity because businesses are no longer bound to their home countries. Transnational
corporations—firms with operations in several countries—now
account for more than 30 percent of the world's total output of
goods and services, and that share is growing by leaps and bounds.

Unlike locally based companies, transnationals can shop around

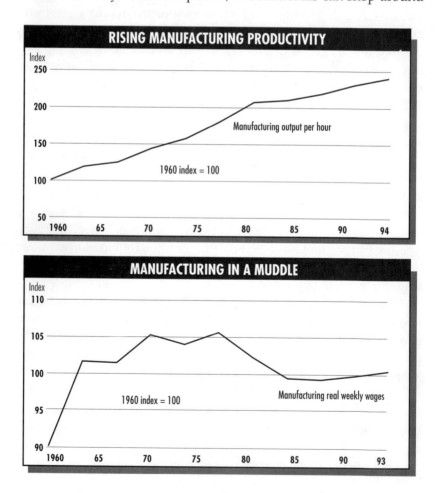

for the cheapest labor worldwide. Since wages are much lower in the developing world, many manufacturers have left big industrial nations like America to set up operations there.

For the manufacturers still operating in the developed world, huge increases in productivity have been absolutely essential to compete with the low-wage countries. But because their costs are so much higher, companies have used productivity gains to lay off workers rather than to produce greater quantities of goods at a higher cost.

Workers are not being rewarded for producing more, which would promote economic growth through greater spending and increased consumer choice. Instead, intense competition from abroad has made them the victims of falling wages, layoffs and depressed living standards.

True, wage competition and rising manufacturing productivity are boosting living standards for lower-level workers in China and other emerging countries where businesses locate. But as wages equalize worldwide, lower-level workers in the United States are seeing their standards of living decline as they are forced to compete with lower-wage Asian workers for jobs.

Unfortunately, there is no obvious short-term remedy for this problem. That's because the discrepancy between the standards of living in the developed world and the undeveloped world is so great. It will probably take several generations for the incomes of manufacturing workers in China and India—whose combined population is roughly eight times that of the United States—to catch up with the incomes of manufacturing workers in the United States. For example, today the wealthiest 20 percent of Chinese and Indians are much less well compensated than the poorest 20 percent of Americans.

Take it from no less than Paul Krugman, the respected Stanford economics professor who happens to be one of the strongest advocates of free trade. Even he is forced to admit that worldwide growth, when accompanied by lower trade barriers, will bring up the standard of living of low-end foreign manufacturing workers at the expense of U.S. manufacturing workers.

Neo-isolationist populists like Pat Buchanan and Ross Perot contend that trade barriers to keep out foreign products would halt the decline in manufacturing wages. The record of protectionism, however, is hardly encouraging. In fact, the Great Depression of the

1930s was in large part triggered by the Smoot-Hawley Act, which was intended to protect U.S. industry.

One reason trade barriers don't work is because they're just like taxes: They slow down overall economic growth and cause prices to increase. Another is they can only delay the inevitable. Attempts to save the U.S. steel industry during the 1970s and '80s, for example, only prolonged an inevitable decline and stalled industry's own efforts to get its house in order.

Just imagine how much more expensive and less safe U.S. cars would be without foreign competition. In short, trade barriers may be tried by vote-hungry politicians in coming years, but they're not a long-term solution to the problem of declining manufacturing wages, a trend that almost certainly has a long way to run.

The Service Sector Squeeze

Worldwide manufacturing productivity increases are hurting, not helping, the typical American worker. But bad as that is, it's only a small part of the overall problem.

The developed world is slowly but surely transforming itself from a manufacturing-based economy to one in which all the major products involve services or information. Most major American exports today are service and information based. The manufacturing sector is becoming an increasingly insignificant part of the economy.

Look at the pie charts, which compare the number of service sector workers to the number of people employed in manufacturing for two periods, 1960 and 1990. In 1960, manufacturing workers—

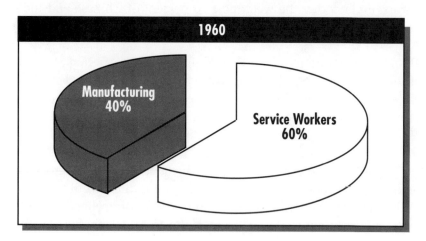

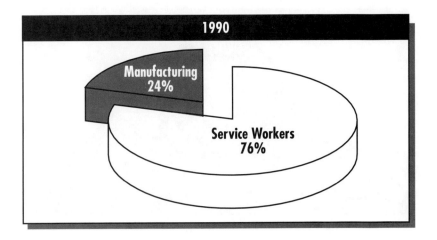

those employed in steelmaking, autos and other industries—accounted for a full 40 percent of the overall workforce, with 60 percent in the service industries. In sharp contrast, by 1990 there were more than three service sector employees in America for every one manufacturing worker.

This quantum shift in the workforce has made service sector productivity far more important to overall living standards. Wealth-enhancing productivity in the service sector—the kind that boosts incomes and living standards—is fundamentally different from that in the manufacturing sector.

The difference is the distinction between quality and quantity. In a manufacturing economy, wealth is increased by producing more. In a service economy, wealth is increased by producing better products and services. Quality, rather than quantity, is what counts.

Recall the ground-breaking work of the humanistic psychologist Abraham Maslow, whose famous pyramid-shaped "hierarchy of needs" is studied in every introductory psychology course in America. The point of the pyramid is to show how people mentally prioritize their various needs.

At the bottom of the pyramid are the most basic human needs, those that must be satisfied first, such as food and shelter. At the top of the pyramid is what people focus on when they've satisfied their basic needs, including such goals as peace of mind and fulfillment of purpose.

At the bottom, the satisfaction of needs can be measured quantitatively. More food is definitely better than less, more shelter prefer-

SERVICE
KNOWLEDGE
PRODUCTS
(books, information)

INDUSTRIAL PRODUCTS
(TVs, VCRs, cars)

AGRICULTURAL PRODUCTS
(food, shelter)

THE MODERN HIERARCHY OF NEEDS

able to less. At the top, however, the key criteria for satisfaction become qualitative. It's no longer enough to have more of something, you want better quality. Personal preference is paramount.

The economy can be thought of similarly. At the lower levels—in the agricultural and industrial sectors—you can measure productivity by how much is produced. The more each worker grows or makes, the richer society becomes. Productivity is purely quantitative.

In the information economy there still are ways to measure productivity quantitatively. But it's debatable whether they measure anything of value, let alone anything that could boost anyone's standard of living.

Consider a service sector worker most of us are familiar with: the bartender. The purely quantitative way to measure his or her productivity would be by the number of drinks poured each hour. But suppose there are just a few customers in the place, all of whom are there just to relax for an hour or so. If the bartender's performance were evaluated purely quantitatively, he or she would have to get each patron dead drunk.

Obviously, pouring more drinks per minute does not make someone a better bartender, any more than writing more pages per minute makes someone a better writer. Instead, knowing the customer, how he likes his martinis or when she might need a sympathetic word, is what really matters. The good bartender is the one most expert in the qualitative and probably unmeasurable aspects of the profession. The reward for that kind of productivity comes in the form of customers' tips.

Computer technology has made possible massive increases in service sector output in the last ten years. For example, brokerage houses can now process many more trades per minute and law firms can crank out countless pages of perfectly polished legal briefs. Unfortunately, neither innovation has anything to do with improving quality.

Take the capability of financial institutions to process more stock market trades in less time. Multibillionaire Warren Buffett is without doubt the most successful investor of our time. But the oracle of Omaha is fond of saying that his favorite holding period is forever. The last thing Buffett needs is the ability to make more transactions. As many investors have learned the hard way, frequent trading in the financial markets is guaranteed to increase your broker's wealth, not your own. In fact, it's generally the surest way to lose money, not a very productive activity.

As for lawyers, their greater "productivity" has buried our legal system and economy under an avalanche of paper. Many prominent jurists have urged national tort reform to deal with the problem. Lawyers' fees? Well, they have buried us as well, and society has footed the bill. That's meant anything but increased social wealth.

The Fruits of Knowledge

Gains in quality are what's important in the service sector. But even they don't increase wealth for everyone. Take it from no less than Peter Drucker, the University of California business professor who is one of the most perceptive commentators on the twentieth-century economy.

According to Drucker, the information society has led to the creation of a new breed of "knowledge workers," the favored few who are able to use their special skills, education or training to create a higher-quality product. Meanwhile, the bulk of workers are becoming increasingly expendable in the eyes of management, which is constantly seeking to replace them through technological advances.

The tools of technology benefit only the knowledge workers. That means the rewards from rising productivity flow to them, at the expense of everyone else. Examples of knowledge workers range from expert traders such as George Soros to baseball all-stars.

What they have in common is unique talents or knowledge that makes them irreplaceable by technological advance.

By speeding up and simplifying the technical aspects of information—such as data transmission, retrieval, and storage—companies can hire fewer service sector workers. That leaves more money to pay the knowledge workers, who are more indispensable than ever. In this way, quantitative productivity gains in the service sector have tilted the balance of power further in favor of knowledge workers.

If all this sounds a bit confusing, it might help to imagine a slightly malevolent Santa Claus, one whose elves toil away year round making toys. Rather than give toys away, this Santa sells them for a profit, paying his elves a certain amount for each toy they make.

With this incentive, the elves continually streamline and improve their operations, producing more toys in less time. Our capitalistic Santa is happy, since he has more toys to sell. The elves are happy, too, since they are making more money. Their increases in productivity translate into bigger paychecks.

Now imagine that times change. Santa's insatiable consumers, the boys and girls who bought his toys, have grown up. They no longer want fire trucks and dolls. Rather, they're now demanding books, new books they have never read before. But whereas before ten trucks or Barbies were better than one, these adult consumers are more discriminating. The books they demand have to be interesting, informative, entertaining. They will rush to buy a great book, but will ignore ten silly books. Quality, not quantity, is key.

Only one of the elves, Sam, has the creative imagination to write entertaining and original books. So now Santa's workers are suddenly split into two groups: on the one hand is the knowledge worker, Sam. On the other are all the other elves, the service workers. Sam creates the books, while the other elves are relegated to typing, assembling and copying whatever Sam puts to pen.

Under this new market reality, the rules in Santa's workshop have changed dramatically. For one thing, it is generating quality, rather than quantity, that counts. On this score, Sam is worth everything while the other elves are expendable. Santa's prime motivation is still to maximize the productivity of the elves. But now productivity has a new meaning. It's no longer measured by the number of toys a single elf can make in a particular period of time. Instead, it's measured in terms of the smallest number of elves needed to copy and bind a particular book.

Who wins? Santa, because he's making more money than ever, and Sam, because he is indispensable. But the other elves will suffer. Those who are lucky enough to keep their jobs will face stagnating incomes and the constant threat of losing their jobs to still more productivity gains.

The elves who do lose their jobs won't sit home forever and collect unemployment. Except during recessions, most will be hired soon afterward. But the jobs they take will almost certainly be lower paying—or at least not higher paying—than the jobs they lost. That's because other companies will also be downsizing to be more competitive, just like Santa. Only if the elves can raise their skills to Sam's level—become knowledge workers—will they have a chance of gaining higher incomes and living standards.

This is exactly how the modern information age workplace is shaping up. Real qualitative productivity is defined in terms of the abilities of a chosen few to turn out a desired product. Those like Sam are Drucker's knowledge workers. The other elves are what Drucker calls service workers. Their productivity can rise, but ultimately it will cost them their jobs and their standard of living.

Moreover, even among knowledge workers—as Robert H. Frank and Philip J. Cook point out in their book, *Winner-Take-All Society*—inequalities are growing. Just take our example to another level to see why. Suppose there were two or three elves capable of writing books. Even if the differences between the best and worst were small, the chances are still great that the best would command a much greater salary. Who, after all, wants to read the second best?

Service sector productivity gains—which in our example would be measured by the number of books turned out per elf—have kept workers' real incomes and living standards in a downtrend, while inequalities continue to widen in the modern world.

Almost every major occupational group within the service sector has experienced a frightening loss of purchasing power that has lasted more than a generation. Look at the graph of the real income of retail workers, for example. Inflation-adjusted, or "real," retail worker wages have been in a free fall since the late 1970s, and there's no end in sight for this alarming trend.

In contrast, consider the astronomical income growth of one typical group of knowledge workers, lawyers. According to Derek Bok,

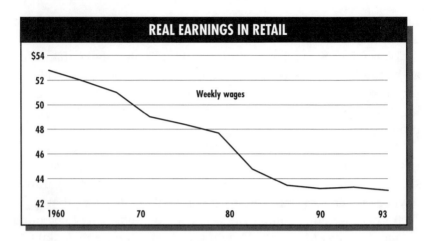

noted author of *The Cost of Talent* and former president of Harvard University, real earnings of the largest law firms soared 20 to 100 percent during the 1970s and 1980s, as Americans became ever more wedded to litigation and paperwork.

The Failure of Technology

Many argue that technology will save the day. The optimists pin most of their hopes on the personal computer, or PC, as the great equalizer. Already, they argue, America's youth has developed computer skills far beyond those of the rest of the world, and even their parents. These skills, they say, will help them enter the knowledge workforce as programmers, writers, businesspeople and a hundred other functions no one has dreamed of yet.

Unfortunately, technological advance in the service sector has up to now been concerned with quantitative productivity boosts. It could take a very long time before gains from technology generate the qualitative gains we really need.

In recent years, technology has been undergoing a miniaturization revolution. About forty years ago, computers took about 18,000 vacuum tubes to perform 5,000 calculations a second. Today computers use microprocessors and integrated circuits, which fit millions of transistors into a space the size of one of those old tubes. In some cases, calculations are performed a million times faster than in the old days.

Information storage capability is one of the prime beneficiaries. Today's CD-ROMs and huge hard drives now make it possible to process and store more information far more quickly than anyone would have dreamed five years ago, and more astronomical advances are on the way.

In a 1994 article, the respected American journal *Science* reviewed the birth of a new, extremely high-potential technology for storing information, called holographic imaging. Holographic imaging is an advance over compact computer disks—which are now capable of storing the entire *Encyclopaedia Britannica*—akin to what compact computer disks were over paper. In other words, holographic imaging will probably be able to store thousands of *Encyclopaedia Britannica*s in just a fraction of the space compact disks now use to store one.

The question is why in the world do we need to store that much information, and does such a capability satisfy existing needs better? Does it add to overall social wealth and help improve living standards?

According to James Glanz, a regular commentator in *Science*, holographic imaging is needed because "the data explosion is straining existing storage technologies." In other words, the current marvels of data storage are no longer adequate to satisfy our needs for rapidly accessible data. Our fantastic ability to store data has simply created a need to store even more data.

Miniaturization has simply created the need for more miniaturization. So far that's the way it has been with most technologies in the information age. Needs are created but never satisfied.

Quantum leaps in technology have quantitatively improved productivity in both the manufacturing and service sectors in recent years. Unfortunately, these physical gains have not produced wealth-enhancing productivity gains to reverse the two-decade–long slide in Americans' real incomes. Benefits of whatever real gains have been generated have gone only to the wealthy. The rest of the population has been left in the dust.

A Turbulent Transition

Will productivity gains again boost workers' wages as during the 1950s and '60s? History says yes, but not for many years. Until then, real wages will keep sinking, inequalities will grow and the cry for growth will ring out loud and clear.

History shows that all epic economic, political and social transitions are wrenching, turbulent affairs—hardly smooth roads to prosperity. The Western world's extremely dislocating change from an agricultural society to an industrial one about a hundred years ago is a good case in point. The massive unemployment and under-employment, wrenching recessions, squalid working conditions and decaying social fabric of the time are well documented by authors such as Theodore Dreiser and Upton Sinclair.

Some of the greatest fortunes of all time were made during those years in everything from oil to autos. The opulence of that period's elite is on display in the massive cliff mansions at Newport, Rhode Island, and is well documented in Gore Vidal's historical novels. Those near the bottom of society, however, didn't begin to enjoy the benefits of increased industrial productivity until the New Deal came about in the 1930s.

The similarities between that time and this are striking. For example, at the same time Bill Gates has become a multibillionaire by dominating the computer software industry, a record number of homeless people have been wandering around America's major cities.

The likely scenario is this: We will eventually learn how to make productivity work for us again, but it will take years. In the mean-time, led by the United States, the cry for growth in the developed world to reverse the slide in incomes will rise to a deafening pitch, even while trade with the developing world is increasing. That will remain a key building block for rising inflation for years to come.

In the next chapter, we look at the other force behind the world's cry for growth—the crisis in education—and how it's hurting rather than helping our efforts to find solutions to the wrenching problems of the day.

3

The Crisis in Education

Education is the key to getting ahead in America. Those who have it get the better jobs and more money. Those who don't, fall behind.

This has never been more true than in the latter 1990s. Developing knowledge worker skills is essential for living a comfortable life in the modern age of information technology and escalating international competition. Doing that means earning at least a college degree, and preferably some graduate study.

During the 1950s and '60s, a college education was also a way to open doors. But even workers with a high school diploma had a chance to succeed back then. That's no longer the case.

Take a look at the graph, which shows income trends, adjusted for inflation, for three groups of workers: those with a college education, those with only a high school diploma and those with eight years or less of schooling.

Since 1981, the paycheck power of high-school–educated workers has fallen 20.87 percent, a far more deadly drop than that of the population as a whole. Incomes of those with an eighth-grade education or less have fallen a depression-like 30.53 percent, relative to inflation. In contrast, college-educated workers' salaries have basically held their own, slipping about 1 percent.

Unfortunately, at the same time that education is more impor-

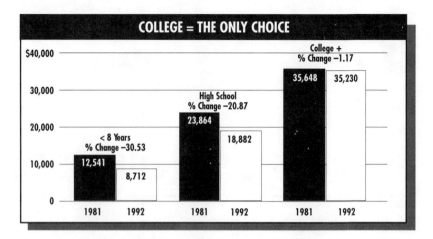

tant than ever, it's harder than ever to get enough of it. In fact, for many people, escalating costs and declining school standards are rapidly closing the only window of opportunity to even keep pace with inflation.

Unable to afford even a college education, a rising number of middle-class youths will be forever trapped in lower-wage jobs that continually lose ground to inflation. As they fall out of the middle class, odds are that their children won't be able to afford higher education either. Their only alternative will be to cry for ever-faster economic growth from their government. The result will be more inflation.

Slumping Standards

Following World War II, the U.S. government made a major commitment to broadening access to education. From the famed GI bill to massive spending for improved grammar schools, federal and state governments made upgrading the public school system a priority.

Public schools did face disruptions following court-ordered racial integration in the 1960s and '70s. But more important, over the past four decades they've graduated an unprecedented number of young Americans who've gone on to attain college and graduate degrees, many from the nation's most elite Ivy League schools.

Unfortunately, the country's public and private schools alike are now faltering in their toughest test: preparing young Americans to become knowledge workers in an increasingly competitive global environment.

The most alarming evidence of this is the almost thirty-year drop in average test scores on college entrance exams, particularly the Scholastic Aptitude Test, or SAT. These tests are used by most colleges to screen for students that have the highest potential for academic success. The higher a student scores on the SAT's logic-based mathematics and verbal tests, the better he or she should perform in college.

The graph "Scary Statistics" tracks the average SAT score of all students taking the tests from 1967 through 1993, the most recent year for which data is available. The average score has fallen fairly consistently year by year to its current level in the 902 area, despite efforts to make the test easier and to better prepare students for it.

This relentless drop in SAT scores shows that students are graduating from high school less prepared for college than they used to be. In addition, the number of students obtaining very high scores has fallen off a cliff. In a recent year, for example, fewer than 1,000 females scored above 750 on the verbal portion of the test.

Why have school standards dropped? For starters, consider this shocking fact: Despite massive expenditures for public and private education over the past three decades, teachers' incomes have fallen below those of manufacturing workers. That's in direct contrast to the pre-1960 era, when teachers made considerably more.

Check out the graph that lists starting salaries of various professions in 1993, and the graph that tracks teachers' salaries from 1971 to 1994. After falling throughout the 1970s, there has been some upward movement in recent years. But new teachers' pay still dramatically trails that of virtually all other occupations. In fact, new

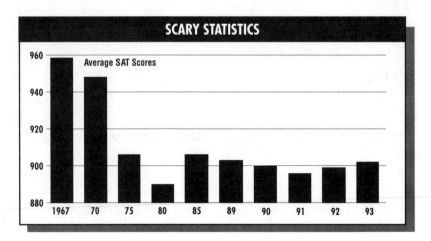

SCARY STATISTICS

Average SAT Scores

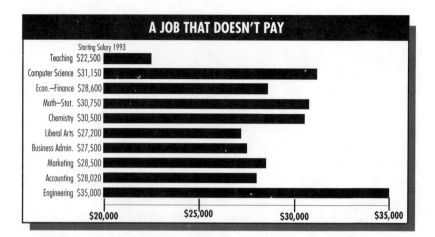

teachers make just a bit more than do most recent high school graduates.

Derek Bok's *The Cost of Talent* lays out the implications of these numbers quite clearly. With little financial incentive to go into teaching, people who years ago would have become educators have instead gone into more lucrative professions, such as medicine, the law or finance. The result has been a shortage of top-notch teachers.

Not surprisingly, SAT scores of teachers have been in a steep decline since the 1960s. In fact, according to some studies, SAT

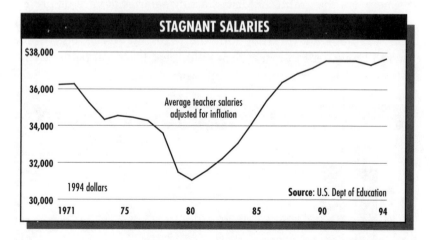

scores of teachers are well below those of the general population. No wonder SAT scores for students have been declining!

The only way to attract the best qualified teachers is to make salaries more competitive with those of other education-intensive positions, such as lawyers and doctors. Unfortunately, the local and state governments that pay for public schools have been hurt by several long-term trends, all of which will continue for some time.

Burden-shifting by the federal government, the flight of industry, erosion of the tax base, decaying infrastructure in the larger cities, the growing costs of social services and other woes have all taken their toll on state and local balance sheets. The drop in municipal creditworthiness is well documented by the dramatic long-term fall in municipal bond prices relative to those of other bonds since the mid-1980s.

Investors have required higher returns to invest in munis. This in turn has boosted governments' costs of borrowing, making it more difficult to finance essential services like public education. Other threats to educational funding include proposals in many states to grant "vouchers" to parents who send their children to private schools. If it becomes widespread, this trend will force public schools to contract even more.

School systems are also plagued by monumental bureaucracies at the elementary, junior high and high school levels. The New York City school budget, for example, recently rang up expenditures of $8,000 per student, only $44 of which were spent on books and classroom materials.

These legions of administrators are intractably connected to local government structures. In most systems, education administrators are the ultimate supervisors of teachers, with the power to hire and fire, even though they contribute little or no actual teaching.

Many administrators are also paid a good deal more than teachers. This has the perverse effect of encouraging the best qualified teachers to become administrators, depriving kids of their expertise and adding to the top-heavy state of the system at the same time.

To be fair, many public school systems, including Washington, D.C.'s, have begun slashing bureaucracy to cut costs. But these structures remain a huge drain on money that's desperately needed for school's biggest job: preparing the country's youth to compete in the internationally competitive information age.

The most intractable reason for the high cost and lesser effectiveness of grammar school education is closely related to the long-term decline in Americans' inflation-adjusted incomes. As both parents have been forced to go to work to pay the bills, teachers have been forced to discipline children more and more, detracting from teaching the "3 Rs."

The need for schools to socialize youngsters has been made even more critical by the trend toward one-parent families. According to some studies, only about half of kids today come from homes with two parents.

The result is a vicious cycle. Dropping real incomes means that parents must work harder and spend less time with their children. This puts the burden on the schools to teach discipline, which detracts from time spent educating. This, in turn, depresses SAT scores and the general quality of education, which makes it more difficult for students to get into colleges and graduate programs.

Fewer qualified students means that fewer knowledge workers will be created to significantly boost qualitative productivity in the economy, and to help American business compete worldwide. Everyone else will fall further behind inflation, as more service sector and manufacturing jobs are lost to downsizing. That will force parents and even their children to work, meaning less time spent socializing children—and so the cycle begins anew.

Out of Reach

Slumping grammar school standards aren't the only barrier to creating more knowledge workers through education. Even the brightest middle- and lower-class kids are being increasingly stymied by the snowballing costs of a college education.

The graph labeled "Out of Reach" shows the percentage of Americans' average family income that has been necessary to finance a student in a private college for one year from 1982 to 1994. Amazingly, the percentage rose from less than 30 percent in 1982 to more than 50 percent in 1994, and it's still increasing. The stunning conclusion: Private college is now out of reach for the average American.

The cost of public colleges has also risen sharply, due in part to dwindling subsidies from state taxpayer dollars. More and more, these schools are billing students for the rising costs of their programs. More ominous, the growing financial instability of the state and local governments that finance these public colleges poses an ongoing threat to current levels of funding. In other words, public colleges are becoming more costly to attend, too.

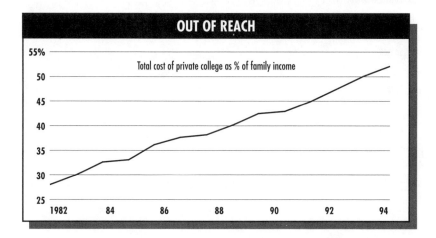

OUT OF REACH

Total cost of private college as % of family income

As the pie chart shows, public universities are extremely dependent on government money. With angry citizens protesting tax increases, forcing politicians to roll back current rates and placing strict limits on raising new money, this support is becoming increasingly scarce.

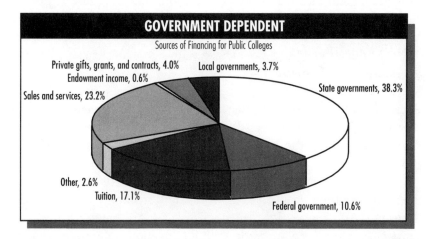

GOVERNMENT DEPENDENT

Sources of Financing for Public Colleges

Private gifts, grants, and contracts, 4.0%   Local governments, 3.7%
Endowment income, 0.6%
Sales and services, 23.2%   State governments, 38.3%
Other, 2.6%
Tuition, 17.1%
Federal government, 10.6%

The problem with bureaucracy is arguably worse at the college level. Here again, power generally resides in a board of directors of sorts, which may or may not include anyone who's ever actually taught students. These boards have exploded the size of college administration at the same time American business has slimmed down.

Each college's army of administrators usually has the power to hire and fire professors. Bureaucratic power is maintained over

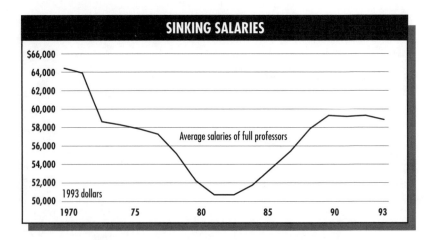

tenured faculty by controlling salaries. This control is well illus-
trated by comparing the growth in average salaries of college professors, from the graph labeled "Sinking Salaries," with the growth
in college tuition.

College professors have not just failed to get a piece of the pie
from rising tuition. Adjusted for inflation, the average full professor—typically a tenured senior employee with a Ph.D.—is making
almost 10 percent less than in 1971, according to the National Center for Educational Statistics. Those with less experience and fewer
credentials have fared worse.

Only full profs at four-year private colleges have seen an
increase in buying power over the past twenty-five years. And for
them, the increase has been less than 10 percent, far less than the
boosts enjoyed by those in any other field requiring similar education.

As a group, college profs are the only knowledge workers that
haven't benefited economically from the transition to the information age. And just as low teachers' salaries are having a negative
impact on the quality of grade school education, colleges' refusal to
pay professors more money is certain to catch up with the quality of
their programs down the road.

What makes this even more dangerous is that the day is fast
approaching when a college education by itself won't be enough to
stay in the American middle class. Go back to the first graph in this
chapter, showing relative salary trends since 1981 for college-
educated workers. Even those with a college degree have seen their
real incomes drop 1.17 percent.

We predict that by early in the next century only a graduate degree will provide the education needed to stay ahead of inflation. Almost everyone else will be faced with a future of losing ground, no matter how many family members join the workforce.

Will colleges be able to provide students with the tools they need to succeed in graduate schools ten years from now? Or will professors' slumping salaries hurt the quality of college education the way low teachers' paychecks are hurting the quality of grade school education today? Either way, college and graduate degrees will continue to cost a great deal of money. Those whose incomes are losing ground to inflation are ill equipped to pay what it takes.

Today, with the cost of a year of college almost 50 percent of an average family's annual income, college is no longer an option for many families. A graduate education is yet another step out of reach.

Less Education = More Inflation

America's educational ills can be fixed. Public and private schools, colleges and universities will have to downsize and shed their red tape. More funds will have to be provided to attract the best teachers and professors, as well as to acquire needed technology. Parents, too, will have to make time in their busy schedules to take greater responsibility for their children.

These are daunting tasks. Though many educational institutions are starting on them now, it will take years to make a real difference. Until then, education will be more a part of America's problems than a solution to them.

Education's failure is certain to close the door of opportunity to many young people in coming years, condemning them to a lifetime of falling behind inflation while the better educated move ahead. They'll form a more or less permanent underclass whose burgeoning ranks will constantly scream for faster economic growth, regardless of inflation. And politicians will leap to obey.

The cry for growth is the first of the three major building blocks of the coming inflation. The next chapter introduces the second: the coming bull market in the basic commodities that go into every industrial product on the planet. Fueled by the emerging demand in the world's developing economies such as China and India, prices of these commodities will rise sharply in coming years, providing major fuel for hotter inflation.

4

The Threat from Abroad

Steel, copper, tin, oil. These basic commodities are used in virtually every product made. Changes in their prices directly impact the price of everything else we buy.

Runaway increases in commodity prices were behind the massive inflation of the 1970s. Stagnant to falling commodity prices were a major force holding inflation in check during the 1980s and early 1990s.

Should commodity prices stay low during the latter 1990s, they'd cool some of the inflationary fire resulting from the cry for growth. The odds of that happening, however, are growing weaker by the day.

Instead, the latter 1990s will mark a return to the commodities bull market of the 1970s, when the price of everything from grains to silver skyrocketed. Rising commodity prices will be the second great building block of the great inflation to come.

What will launch this bull market? The insatiable demand for these basic commodities in the world's developing economies.

The greatest external threat to America's economic security is not Japan, Russia, China or even Iran. It's our growing dependence on imported steel, copper, tin, energy and other commodities that are the basic building blocks of all other products and services. Almost everything we eat, read, drive, hear, see or taste is made from commodities in some form. Without them, our economy simply could not exist.

As we enter the twenty-first century, the United States is by far the world's biggest consumer of basic commodities. The more our economy expands, the more of them we need. But in contrast to earlier times, we no longer produce all of the commodities we need. Despite tremendous improvements in productivity and innovations in recycling and conservation, a rising share of our raw materials is coming from abroad. Sources range from stable countries like Canada and Australia to politically shaky regimes in Africa and Latin America.

There are two problems with this arrangement. Both add up to higher inflation in the latter 1990s. First, the developed world is no longer the globe's only consumer of commodities.

Even as the United States, Europe and Japan struggle for supremacy in the dawning information age of the twenty-first century, less developed nations on every continent are striving to raise living standards. Many are struggling to shift from rural agrarian societies to full-fledged industrial nation-states. In the process, they're consuming ever-greater amounts of commodities, much of which they must import.

The more these countries demand, the more competition American companies will face for basic commodities. That will put considerable upward pressure on commodity prices for years to come. Because commodities are used in virtually every product, those higher costs will boost prices of almost everything. The inescapable result: higher inflation.

The second danger of our growing dependence on foreign commodities is politically based. As sources of copper, tin, steel and other building blocks become more far-flung, their supply will become ever more vulnerable to interruptions, which will trigger price spikes.

We've seen examples of this already. For instance, strikes and breakdowns in Nigeria's copper mines put upward pressure on copper prices for much of 1994 and well into 1995. Our increasing dependence on imported commodities places us at growing risk of politically triggered upward price spikes in these essential items.

The decline of the U.S. dollar in recent years has put us at risk of giving up control over the channels of commodity distribution as well. It's even possible that basic commodities like oil—which today is priced in U.S. dollars—may some day be calculated in another currency, such as the Japanese yen. Should this happen, drops in the dollar alone would trigger corresponding increases in commodity prices.

As our graph shows, rising commodity prices have been a pre-cursor to every upswing in inflation in the post–World War II period. The graph compares the twelve-month rates of change in an index of basic raw materials—the All Commodity Producer Price Index (ACPPI)—with those of the Consumer Price Index (CPI), which gauges changes in prices of finished goods.

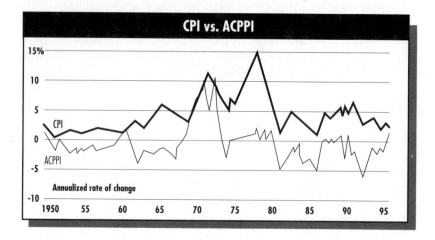

Even though commodity prices account for only about 10 per-cent of the CPI, they are generally followed by moves in the overall rate of inflation. In fact, every time the ACPPI has risen more than 1 percent over a twelve-month period, the result has been a spike up in inflation on the consumer level.

Political uncertainty, escalating worldwide demand and slumping supply make higher commodity prices a surety over the next ten to fifteen years. The importance of commodities to the economy makes their coming bull market the second building block for the coming inflation.

1970s Déjà Vu

In the 1970s, a group of scientists and various luminaries known as the Club of Rome issued a now infamous report on the state of the world's resources. Its conclusion—which was based on then-current growth rates in demand—was that the world was running out of basic commodities, and would face a series of destabilizing short-ages in future years.

13 RAW INDUSTRIALS			
Commodities	**Features**	**Material traded**	**Pricing**
Burlap	10 oz., 40"	N.Y.	cents/yd
Copper scrap	#2	N.Y.	cents/lb
Cotton	1-1/16, (7 market avg.)	N.Y.	cents/lb
Hides	heavy native	Central U.S.	cents/lb
Lead scrap	heavy soft		cents/lb
Print cloth	48", 78 x 78	N.Y.	cents yd
Rosin	window glass	N.Y.	$/cwt
Rubber	#1 rib smoke sheet	N.Y	cents/lb
Steel scrap	#1 heavy melting	Chicago	$/ton
Tallow	prime	Chicago	cents/lb
Tin	grade A	N.Y.	cents/lb
Wool Tops	nominal	Boston	cents/lb
Zinc	prime Western	N.Y.	cents/lb

Source: Bureau of Labor Statistics Commodities

At the time, the theory certainly seemed plausible. Prices of everything from grain to tin were rising through the roof. Rapidly expanding economies the world over were sucking in ever-rising amounts of raw materials. Meanwhile, political turmoil was threatening supplies in Africa and Latin America, triggering periodic upward price spikes. This state of affairs continued for most of the 1970s.

The falling commodity prices of the past fifteen years make the Club of Rome's conclusions seem a bit ridiculous. The recession of the early 1980s inaugurated a period of slower economic growth, with a far reduced demand for basic commodities. At the same time, the higher prices of the 1970s provided a powerful incentive to raise productivity and discourage wasteful use of basic products. New reserves of minerals were discovered, even in developed nations.

The result has been a breakdown in the prices of most major commodities over the past ten to fifteen years. Today, despite a rally in 1994 and early 1995, most are as cheap as they've ever been, adjusted for inflation. For example, energy was cited in the club's report as a commodity we could run out of altogether. But as you can see from our graph, energy prices—represented by oil—are actually at twenty-year lows, adjusted for inflation. In fact, they've lost ground even if you don't take inflation into account.

The collapse in commodity prices has laid the groundwork for

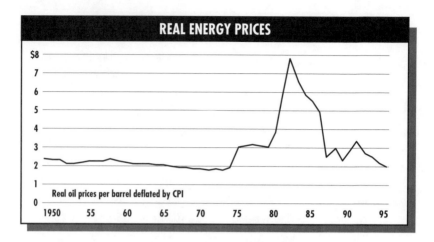

their recovery in the latter 1990s. Indications are that this boom could dwarf that of the 1970s.

The world's attitude toward commodities today is much the same as it was during the 1960s. In that bygone era, there seemed to be no end to the world's potential sources of raw materials to fuel ever-increasing economic growth. Industries paid little or no heed to how much tin or copper they used in making machinery, automobiles or anything else. Cheap energy was considered a God-given right, as most Americans drove eight-cylinder gas guzzlers that were lucky to get ten miles per gallon of gasoline.

In the mid-1990s, even the biggest cars generally get at least fifteen to twenty miles per gallon, a function both of more efficient engines and less steel being used in their construction. Further progress toward more efficient usage of commodities is, however, most decidedly out of favor.

At the height of the 1970s energy crisis, President Jimmy Carter urged Americans to wear sweaters indoors to save electricity. In contrast, we're now turning down our thermostats in summer and ratcheting them up in winter. Inefficient, wasteful use of commodities is most decidedly on the rise.

The increase in the developed world's demand for commodities is just a drop in the bucket compared to what's going on in the developing world. China's economy, for example, was growing at a double-digit rate in mid-1995, despite the government's attempt to rein in inflation.

As trade analyst Paul Krugman points out, Chinese growth is

not coming from gains in productivity. Instead, it's a result of the country's transition from an agrarian society to an industrial one. Traditional farms generally use few commodities. But even efficient, well-constructed industrial plants use a wealth of them. Consequently, the mere transition itself is triggering a literal explosion in Chinese demand for commodities.

The fact that Chinese factories are rarely very efficient has boosted demand even more. At last count, China consumed five times as much energy for the same amount of output as the typical U.S. company and twelve times as much as the ultraefficient Japanese. Put another way, every increase in Chinese production requires twelve times the energy as the same increase in Japan.

Consequently, the so-called Asian miracle has been nothing more than the successful marshaling of enormous resources almost without regard to how productively the resources are used.

Our bar chart shows projected growth in demand for energy in China and India to 2020. Already net importers of energy, these countries' appetites for oil, gas and other fuels will clearly be a major force pushing prices upward in the years ahead. The same trend will be repeated for commodities from A to Z.

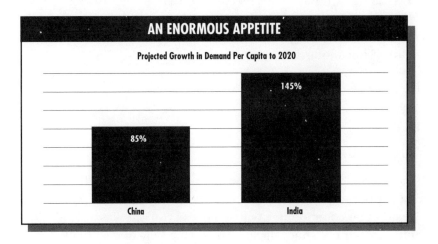

AN ENORMOUS APPETITE

Projected Growth in Demand Per Capita to 2020

China — 85%
India — 145%

Recent estimates from the Asia-Pacific Economic Cooperation (APEC) organization forecast that China's imports of oil will quintuple by 2010 to over 3 million barrels per day. That's fully one-half of Saudi Arabia's current production and 15 percent of total global consumption, more than three times today's levels.

With nearly one-quarter of the world's population housed within its borders, China is the largest developing nation making the move from an agricultural to an industrial power. However, it's by no means the only nation making the jump. India, the world's second most populous country, is also on the go. Ditto for would-be powerhouse Indonesia, and for the economic "tigers" of Southeast Asia.

The developing economies of Asia already consume some 25 percent of the world's annual demand for basic commodities. As we enter the new millennium, their needs will grow in tandem with their explosive national growth rates. As the table shows, Asian economies continue to grow at several times the rate of the United States. That should significantly up their share of world demand.

With the world crying out for faster economic growth to reverse the downtrend in inflation-adjusted, or real, incomes, both the developed and developing world will suck down ever-rising amounts of everything from antimony to zinc to fuel their progress in coming years. That alone is a sure-fire prescription for rising commodity prices well into the next century.

THE SIZZLING SEVEN		
	Annual Growth Rate	
	1980	1990
South Korea	3.5%	8%
Hong Kong	9.0	9
Indonesia	9.3	7
Malaysia	8.0	7
Philippines	5.2	4
Taiwan	6.4	8
Thailand	6.3	7

Source: *Strategic Atlas*, 3rd ed., HarperPerennial

Supply Squeeze

The other side of the rising commodity price equation is the growing supply squeeze throughout the world. The Club of Rome's conclusion that commodities will somehow run out was always highly unlikely. Supply shortfalls always have a way of eventually reversing themselves, as the experience of the 1970s and '80s proved.

Unfortunately, supply surpluses practically guarantee eventual shortages. The key is the incentive to produce. Low commodity prices are a powerful disincentive for producers to seek new reserves or deposits. Companies instead try to boost profits by squeezing market share from competitors. Only higher prices will boost profit margins enough to induce companies to rev up their exploration and production (E&P) budgets.

The supply shortfalls of the 1970s were in large part ended by the massive E&P budgets they encouraged. Buoyed by rising revenue from existing production, companies could afford to plow far larger sums into discovering and exploiting new reserves of commodities. Higher prices also encouraged production from higher-cost existing reserves. All this together dramatically increased supplies of everything from aluminum to zinc, which eventually reversed the imbalance of supplies relative to demand. This stymied the advance of prices, and later speeded their decline.

Similarly, falling prices over the past ten years or so have dramatically cut profit margins for commodity producers. Even for the strongest companies—such as copper magnate Phelps Dodge and Freeport McMoRan—this has led to less extensive, far more focused E&P, and cutbacks in production. Many of the weaker commodity producers have been run out of business, and others are on the brink of bankruptcy, unable to ratchet up production even if they wanted to.

Production of most basic raw materials has, therefore, at best stagnated in recent years. Coupled with the rise in demand for commodities in both the developing and developed world, this is starting to reverse the supply-demand equation in favor of higher prices.

Ultimately, higher prices for basic materials will alter the supply-demand relationship once again, sending prices tumbling. But that's a long way off.

Commodity price cycles tend to be very long term in nature. The main reason is the tremendous amount of time it takes to discover, locate and exploit enough new sources of most industrial commodities to have a significant impact on supply. Once a company closes a facility or is run out of business, it can take years before others make up for the shortfall. The delay is even more pronounced when it comes to developing new reserves or to building expensive new refineries or plants.

Take the example of the steel industry over the past two decades. Cheaper foreign competition, boosted by lower labor costs, leveled the once powerful American companies during the 1970s and early 1980s. Republican and Democratic presidents alike tried in vain to shore up the failing industry, using everything from government aid to trade war threats against foreign steel exporters like Japan. None of their efforts could stop or even slow down what seemed to be a permanent state of downsizing for steel, regardless of the health of the economy.

America wasn't the only country where lower prices were contracting steel production. By the late 1980s, falling prices had triggered a downsizing even in the foreign exporting nations. Today, much of the world's production comes from superefficient "mini-mills," which can control their output to meet changes in demand.

Mini-mill steel companies like Nucor and Oregon Steel still experience fluctuations in profits from upturns and downturns in the economy and demand for steel. However, their profit volatility is far less than that of the big steel producers of the past like U.S. Steel. The drawback is that they produce considerably less steel.

Aside from the mini-mills, lower steel prices have discouraged companies from building big new plants, or even from keeping many old ones going. The steel-making labor force has shrunk dramatically, and the industry as a whole wields nowhere near the clout it did in the 1960s, when President John F. Kennedy won kudos from the public—and panicked the stock market—by attempting to break up alleged price collusion between the largest steel companies.

As a result, as our graph shows, there's less steel-making capacity today than there was in the late 1970s. In fact, America's ability to produce steel is now 26.4 percent less than it was in 1980!

This has sown the seeds for a long-term uptrend in steel prices. Faster economic growth around the world is already pushing up

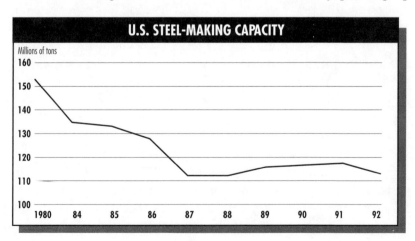

U.S. STEEL-MAKING CAPACITY

Millions of tons

demand, especially in developing nations, which are building infrastructure as they move from agrarian to industrial economies. But years of falling prices have kept new steel plants from coming on line. That makes increases in new steel-making capacity unlikely until prices have risen for some time, possibly several years.

The same thing holds true for production of other commodities, where low prices have restricted supplies. It will take the promise of some awfully big profits to induce commodity-producing countries or companies to spend money on enough new production to really impact supplies. That kind of money just isn't around when prices are low as they are today. Consequently, when prices do start heading up, there will be a considerable lag before new production starts coming onstream. In fact, it could be years before enough comes on line to have a real effect on prices.

The experience of the 1970s and '80s also shows that it can take years of higher prices before conservation and switching to alternatives have a real effect on reducing demand. As a result, once set in motion, commodity prices can rise for years before reversing course. That's exactly where we stand now.

How high can commodity prices go in coming years? Take a look at our chart labeled "A Long Bear Market," which compares 1993 prices of the most widely used raw materials with their prices in 1980. As our chart shows, only zinc has been able to push on to higher highs. Most commodities today sell at prices that are well

A LONG BEAR MARKET			
Commodity	Average Price 1980	Average Price 1993	% Change
Titanium	$126.37	$40.00	-68.35
Copper	101.00	92.00	-8.91
Platinum	677.00	370.00	-45.35
Silver	20.63	4.20	-79.64
Lead	42.50	32.00	-24.71
Tin	846.00	385.00	-54.49
Zinc	37.40	46.00	22.99
Sulfur	89.06	32.00	-64.07
Coal	24.52	23.00	-6.20
Petroleum	21.59	14.23	-34.09
Average			-36.28

below their levels of the boom times, despite a strong rally during the past two years. Relative to inflation, prices are positively depressionary.

It's no wonder much of the commodity-producing industry is mired in a massive depression. It may take years to restore former production levels for many commodities, let alone meet the explosive worldwide demand that's just starting to kick in.

Given our starting point this time around, it's very possible we'll see prices of many commodities rise well above the highs they set back in the late 1970s and early 1980s. Because commodities are used in everything, that means higher inflation well into the next century.

Political Perils

Perhaps the most compelling argument for higher commodity prices is the political danger of America's increasing dependence on foreign sources. Specifically, the questions of where raw materials will come from, who will control their production and whether their supply can be relied on will be increasingly important to their prices. If one or more of these three factors look suspect, it could trigger a violent upward price spike, with a corresponding jump in inflation.

When we entered the industrial age at the turn of this century, the United States was blessed with an abundance of basic commodities. Cheap and plentiful raw materials gave industry a major leg up on foreign competitors as the economy moved from an agrarian to an industrial age.

As we enter the twenty-first century and the information age, America is still blessed with an abundance of oil and natural gas, copper, iron, lead, silver, zinc, aluminum and a host of agricultural products. Unfortunately, our economy has grown to the point where our wealth of resources is no longer enough to handle our appetite for them. Consequently, we're now importing more of these vital economic building blocks than ever before.

Our table labeled "Growing Dependence" tells the story. By 1993, America was more than 50 percent dependent on foreign sources for seventeen major commodities that were once almost entirely drawn from domestic sources. We were 100 percent dependent for five. Of the twenty-one commodities listed in the table, imports made up 69 percent of our supplies, compared with 54 percent in 1960.

			GROWING DEPENDENCE	

Mineral or Metal	1960*	1993*	Major Uses
Niobium	100%	100%	Nuclear reactors, high-strength steel products
Manganese	89	100	Essential in hardened, corrosion-resistant steel products
Mica Sheet	94	100	Electrical condensers, optical instruments, general purpose insulator
Strontium	100	100	Treatment of bone cancer, long-lasting power sources
Bauxite	74	100	Principal component of aluminum
Platinum	82	88	Indispensible in many chemical processes
Tantalum	94	86	Steel products, semiconductors
Tungsten	32	84	Wide variety of electronic devices, rocket engines
Chromium	85	82	Electrical protective coatings
Tin	82	81	Essential packaging material, electroplating
Cobalt	66	75	Glass and steel manufacturing
Potash	0	71	Electrical and thermal insulator
Cadmium	13	66	Protection of precision parts
Nickel	72	64	Stainless steel
Barite	74	58	Oil and gas drilling
Antimony	43	57	Semiconductors, chemical tnaks, batteries
Petroleum	17	50	Most important source of energy
Selenium	25	46	Photoelectric devices
Sulfur	0	15	Food preparation, chemistry laboratories
Iron & Steel	0	12	Widespread in all types of construction
Copper	0	6	Electrical industries, home building
Unweighted Average	54	69	

*Percent of U.S. demand imported.

Part of the reason we're living beyond our commodity means is that there are cheaper deposits of minerals and other raw materials in other countries. In other words, some of our commodity reserves are capable of meeting our needs. It just doesn't make sense to use them if we can obtain the same resources more cheaply outside this country.

But whatever the cause, the result is the same. Except for grains and other foodstuffs—of which the United States remains one of the world's dominant producers—America is becoming increasingly dependent on imported commodities to maintain its economic health. That makes us more and more vulnerable to any sort of instability elsewhere in the world that can affect the supply or the price of commodities we need.

If we're not producing the commodities we use, who is? It

depends on what raw material you're talking about. Copper, for example, is found in places ranging from democratic and economically stable Chile to largely anarchic Zaire. South Africa is the world's top producer of a wide range of minerals, including diamonds and chromium. Russia contains vast reserves of some sixteen vital minerals, while Australia and Canada each have a dozen.

Most of the time, most of these countries are more or less stable, both economically and politically speaking. Also, even if all hell is breaking loose politically and economically, their governments will try to keep their mines running to generate vital foreign exchange. Consequently, the world can usually count on a steady supply of needed commodities. And with the ethos of capitalism spreading around the globe, most commodity-producing countries are anxious to exploit their mineral wealth to fuel their own economic growth.

Unfortunately, the experience of recent years proves that foreign commodity supplies can't always be counted on. Chile's nationalization of Anaconda's copper mine holdings in the early 1970s is one example. The breakdown of the Zairian copper mines in 1994 is another. And once a supply of commodities is interrupted, even temporarily, the result is almost always a major spike up in prices and often in the overall inflation rate.

Several major producers of commodities are suspect today. In the oil-rich Middle East, political turmoil caused by anti-Western Islamic fundamentalism and severe economic inequalities is a constant threat to regimes from Morocco to Saudi Arabia. Both Iran and Iraq have huge military establishments on the Persian Gulf, the world's oil lifeline. As the Gulf War of 1990 proved, any turbulence would have an immediate effect on oil prices. Any permanent political change could have a monster effect.

South Africa recently elected its first multiracial government. President Nelson Mandela has pledged to develop the country rapidly. Since his success will depend to a large degree upon generating foreign exchange, keeping the country's commodity exports up to speed is crucial. If the economic development goals are not met, however, poorer black and white South Africans may lose patience with Mandela's gradualist approach. Even if they don't, Mandela won't live forever. His successor may not be as friendly to foreigners.

Consequently, there's still a chance that commodity flows from South Africa could be interrupted at some point in the future. That also goes for the production of other African nations, most of which are far less stable politically and economically than South Africa. Zaire, for example, is the source of almost half of the world's cobalt. That country continues to be largely ungovernable.

The Russian Threat

The biggest wild card among major world commodity producers is the old Soviet Union, particularly Russia, which remains a major source of many vital commodities (see table). Russia's democratic government has thus far survived a variety of challenges. Unfortunately, the country's economic woes continue to be quite severe.

The government has enjoyed some success in its efforts to attract foreign investors and privatize certain industries. However, inflation is still running out of control and economic growth has actually been negative. Worse, much of the population remains dependent on the huge, bloated bureaucracy. Some believe it's only a matter of time before democracy succumbs to a challenge it won't be able to stare down.

For major users of commodities, like the United States, there has been one fortunate side effect of Russia's crisis: The country's dire economic straits have forced it to raise as much foreign exchange as it can. That's meant selling its vast reserves of minerals and other natural resources. These huge surpluses have been a major factor keeping down commodity prices in general.

It's highly unlikely, however, that the country will continue to export at the current feverish rate indefinitely. First, much of Russia's infrastructure for mining, drilling and production of its existing raw material reserves is quite ancient and in desperate need

VITAL RESOURCES IN THE OLD SOVIET UNION

	% World Production
Iron	28.0%
Cobalt	13.0
Chrome	37.5
Manganese	39.0
Molybdenum	11.0
Nickel	24.0
Tungsten	17.0
Vanadium	30.5
Bauxite	5.5
Copper	12.0
Tin	15.0
Lead	17.0
Zinc	17.0
Silver	14.5
Platinum	48.0
Antimony	12.0
Mercury	32.5
Coal	19.0
Oil	11.0

Source: *Strategic Atlas*, 3rd ed., HarperPerennial

of upgrading. Bureaucratic roadblocks have prevented foreign capital from financing many improvements and the country itself is not capable of making them. If the situation does not change, Russia will have no choice but to cut back on production. Exploration for new reserves is even more difficult, given capital needs and the problems with securing permits for development.

Second, should Russia begin to get back on its feet, it's certain to reduce its commodity exports because of increased domestic demand for resources. A healthier economy will also reduce the desperate need for foreign exchange, making it wiser to stockpile to take advantage of higher prices ahead. In addition, if things don't improve, risks will grow that the country will choose a different economic course, one that involves stockpiling commodities instead of aiming to export to the max.

The bottom line is that the Russian supply boom for commodities is not likely to last into the next century. Once it ends, it will further shift the supply-demand balance in favor of higher prices for raw materials, from manganese to lead and platinum. And, if political turmoil erupts, the upshot could be severe upward price spikes and tremendous inflationary pressures.

A Question of Control

Even if the political situation remains stable in commodity-producing nations, America's dependency on imported commodities still poses a threat. The reason: growing control over the world's remaining commodity resources by foreign-based multinationals.

The major force at work here is the continuing decline of the U.S. dollar. The greenback slipped from a high of around 240 yen/dollar in 1984 to a low of 80 in mid-1995, before bouncing back over 100 recently. Declines almost as massive have been posted against the German mark and other European currencies over that same period of time.

At first glance, this trend may not seem so bad. After all, a falling dollar means that U.S. exports are cheaper and more competitive all over the world. A paycheck paid with dollars costs a company far less than one paid with yen or marks. The going has been made considerably easier for U.S. firms that are going head-to-head with Japanese and European firms in world markets, as well as in the United States.

To compete, Japanese companies have had to cut prices and let profits fall. That's a major reason why the Japanese economy flirted with a recession in the mid-1990s while most other developed world economies were off and running for some time.

The Japanese, however, have played one of the oldest and most successful economic games around: suffering short-term pain for the promise of tremendous long-term gains. The high yen is providing a once-in-a-lifetime opportunity for Japanese multinationals to buy up the world's production capacity for commodities on the cheap, particularly in fast-growing, high-potential Asia.

The currencies of most developing world economies where commodities are produced are linked in varying degrees to the U.S. dollar. When the yen goes up against the greenback, it buys more in those countries. As a result, Japanese companies can afford to buy, say, more steel-producing plants in Asia than competing U.S. companies can.

Our table labeled "Dollar Doldrums" illustrates this in more detail. Suppose that in mid-1994, an American, a German and a Japanese company each had enough money raised to buy one factory in a particular Asian economy. The table shows what percentage of the factory each country could buy in mid-1995, based on exchange rate trends over that time.

Just one year later, the Americans would be able to buy slightly less than the whole factory, while the Japanese would be able to buy one and a third factories. The Germans would be able to buy one and a quarter factories. The effect is that American companies like Du Pont and Primerica have canceled foreign investment projects in recent years, while Japanese and other strong currency countries are inexorably moving their manufacturing to foreign soils. Put another way, in the battle over who will control the world supplies for increasingly scarce vital commodities, the Japanese and Germans have a leg up on everyone else, including U.S. companies.

DOLLAR DOLDRUMS

Percent of a Factory Currencies Buy in Mid-1995
in the Pacific Rim vs. Year Before

	Dollars	Marks	Yen
China	97%	125%	131%
Hong Kong	100	129	136
India	100	129	136
Indonesia	103	133	140
Malaysia	90	117	122
Philippines	95	123	129
Singapore	88	113	119
South Korea	94	122	128
Taiwan	96	124	130

What does this mean for world commodity prices? One particularly horrifying possibility is that these vital raw materials could eventually be priced in another currency, such as the Japanese yen. Currently, most commodities are still priced mostly in U.S. dollars, so a drop in the dollar doesn't usually push up their prices, and by extension U.S. inflation. But if oil and copper, for example, were priced in yen, any change in the dollar would have an effect on their prices, and therefore inflation.

At any rate, the commodity buyout by our Japanese rivals does not augur good things for American inflation. As long as the U.S dollar slips and slides, our control over the channels of commodity distribution will be at increasing risk.

Hot Commodities

Soaring demand for commodities in the developed and developing world, shrinking supplies due mostly to today's low prices, the improbability of new production without significant price increases, the instability of world producers, the growing dependence of the United States on foreign sources of natural resources and the buy-out of resources by nations with stronger currencies augur higher commodity prices in the years ahead for the United States and other nations as well.

And once the trend is in motion it's certain to continue for years to come. Combined with the cry for faster economic growth that we analyzed in the first three chapters, that adds up to a pretty compelling case for higher inflation in coming years. Now let's match these long-term forces together with the third major building block of the coming inflation: our huge monetary and debt overhang.

5

Too Much Money

Here's a trivia question: Which developed country suffered the worst inflation during this century? Answer: Germany in 1923.

Bankrupted by World War I and harassed by the victorious allies for war reparations, Germany faced a crippling combination of heavy debt, a damaged industrial base, rising unemployment and scarce capital by the early 1920s. To pump up growth, the German government began making cheap loans to banks and gave out money to industry in order to maintain payrolls.

That proved to be the wrong move at the wrong time. As Charles P. Kindleberger writes in his book *The World in Depression, 1929–1939*, already-rapid inflation became hyperinflation by 1923. The value of the German mark fell from 7,000 per U.S. dollar in January to some 4.2 trillion per dollar by November of that year.

The inflationary fires were quenched in 1924 when the newly independent German central bank introduced deflationary policies, such as the launching of a new gold-backed currency. The cure, however, was no less painful than the disease. After 1924, bankruptcies became increasingly common, especially for companies that had borrowed during the inflation. Unemployment skyrocketed.

The combination of hyperinflation and harsh deflationary policies to bring it under control effectively destroyed the German middle class. More than anything else, that disaster made possible the rise of Adolf Hitler.

What makes this relevant to late-twentieth-century America? As scholars Andrea Sommariva and Giuseppe Tullio—authors of *German Macroeconomic History 1880–1979*—point out, the great German inflation had earlier roots: the German government's massive printing of money to jump-start economic growth after World War I and the rising inflationary expectations of the early 1920s.

By 1923, Germany was awash with money. So when the government tried to give away money to rev up economic growth, it was the spark that ignited the inflationary powder keg. As Sommariva and Tullio point out, "The growth of money and prices in 1921 and 1922 may suggest that monetary policy could not be considered responsible for the resumption of domestic inflation and exchange rate depreciation. . . . [H]owever, a large monetary overhang was inherited from the war period so that slight changes in expectations of inflation were sufficient . . . to bring about a depreciation of the exchange rate and an acceleration of domestic inflation."

Like 1920s Germany, America in the late 1990s also has a severe monetary overhang. Since the recession of 1990, the Federal Reserve has pumped up the country's money supply—the total amount of currency in circulation along with bank deposits and other liquid assets. Americans have borrowed money in record amounts and have made huge investments in the financial markets.

Unlike 1920s Germany, we have a generally healthy economy and a relatively low rate of inflation, at least for the moment. Consequently, it's difficult to conceive that inflation will get as far out of control as it did in post–World War I Germany. Nonetheless, given the large amount of money floating around in our economy now, it wouldn't take much of a spark of inflationary expectations to set off an inflation explosion.

Our huge monetary and debt overhang is the third major building block for the coming inflation. Together with the cry for growth and the coming bull market in basic commodities, it spells sharply higher inflation in the years ahead, and turmoil for the financial markets.

Daunting Debt

As a rule, the best way to measure monetary overhang is by gauging the rate of growth in the money supply. Money supply is a crude attempt to measure all cash in the economy. High rates of growth over a long period of time create monetary overhang, low rates of growth eliminate it.

There are several different official measures of money supply, each including and excluding certain types of cash. Today's world is characterized by rapidly changing financial innovations and preferences. What's a significant source of cash today may be obsolete tomorrow, just as insignificant sources now can be critical at another time.

During the early 1990s, for example, the Federal Reserve printed money overtime to save the wobbly U.S. banking system. It took a long time, however, for that aggressive action to boost the growth of the overall economy. The reason: the money was being invested in the stock market rather than in conventional interest-paying bank deposits.

The most dangerous form of monetary overhang is debt. Total debt—including government debt—is the broadest measure of money and credit that the Federal Reserve reports in its *Flow of Funds* statistics.

Today, with more cash in their pockets, confident consumers are borrowing more to finance purchases. Total consumer debt is flirting with record levels. As our graph shows, it's also rising steadily relative to our Gross National Product (GNP), which measures the entire economic output of the country. In fact, current levels are the highest since the Great Depression of the 1930s.

Alarmed by the growth of debt in the economy, both Democrats and Republicans are now engaged in a battle to balance the federal

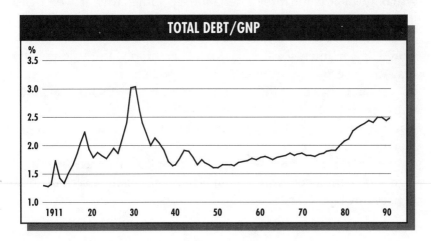

TOTAL DEBT/GNP

budget. The only argument now seems to be who can do the most the quickest. Few have questioned the premise that federal budget balancing will be a panacea for our economic problems and eliminate monetary overhang.

Unfortunately, it won't do much of either. As our pie chart shows, total government debt is only about a third of the total debt in the economy. The current annual federal budget deficit of $160–170 billion is only about one-thirtieth of that. So, even if the federal budget were completely balanced today, it would do little to reduce the monetary overhang.

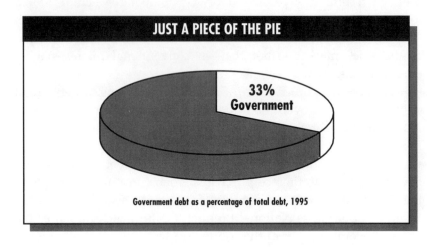

JUST A PIECE OF THE PIE

33%
Government

Government debt as a percentage of total debt, 1995

Efforts to cut spending or raise taxes to balance the budget will pull money out of the economy. At best, this will only slow the economy, or it could prove deflationary. Either way, it won't ease the country's debt burden by much.

Some economists argue that reducing federal budget deficits would lower interest rates, at least temporarily, outweighing the drag on the economy from big budget cuts. The record, however, is not encouraging. Even the 3 percent interest rates that prevailed for much of 1993 failed to reverse America's generation-long decline in real incomes. In fact, they actually added to the growth of debt and monetary overhang.

Whether or not the federal government does balance its budget, high total debt levels will remain. That will remain a serious inflationary threat.

Pricey Stocks

Another symptom of monetary overhang is the sky-high stock prices of the mid-1990s. Since dropping to the low 2000s during the Persian Gulf Crisis of 1990/91, the Dow Jones Industrial Average has doubled and then some. Other major stock market averages have pushed relentlessly upward. Stocks today are at their most expensive levels in history, relative to the corporate earnings that ultimately determine their value.

The best way to measure the relationship between stock prices and profits is the price-to-earnings ratio (P/E). It's calculated by dividing a stock's price by its annual earnings per share of stock. For example, a company earning $4 per share and with a stock price of $40 a share would have a P/E of 10 ($40/$4). The higher a stock's P/E, the more expensive it is relative to its earnings.

The P/E of Standard & Poor's index of the 400 largest industrial companies (S&P 400) is the best gauge of how cheap or dear the overall stock market is. Our graph tracks the S&P 400 P/E since 1960, using a five-year average to factor out year-to-year fluctuations. Our figures also use cash flow earnings, to factor out one-time events like write-offs and give a more accurate picture of earnings. Conclusion: Stocks have never been more expensive than they are today. In fact, they're more expensive than they were during the 1960s—on the eve of the last great bear market.

It takes a great deal of money to push stocks to such lofty levels. Today's high P/Es therefore indicate a great deal of liquidity—or monetary overhang—in the economy. In recent years, consumers

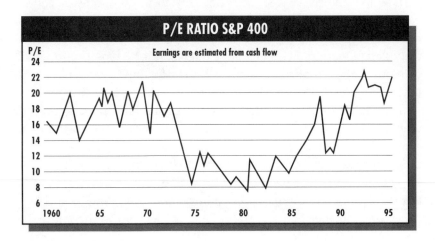

P/E RATIO S&P 400

have had increasing amounts of cash on their hands. They've invested much of it in mutual funds, which in turn have plowed these dollars into stocks and bonds, forcing prices upward. Higher stock market valuations are a clear indication that there is more money in the economy.

From the late 1980s through the first half of the 1990s, high P/Es show that the market has remained much more overvalued than during any other period on which we have data on U.S. stocks. Thus the American economy today has more monetary overhang, or liquidity, than ever before.

P/Es aren't the only measure of stock values that has reached an historic high. Dividend yields, which measure companies' dividends as a percentage of their stock prices, are at record low levels. Price-to-book value ratios, which compare stock prices with companies' net worths (assets minus liabilities), are near all-time highs.

Slowing the Car

One of the major jobs of the Federal Reserve is to mop up the excess liquidity that creates sky-high stock market valuations. But with P/Es as high as they are now, the task is all but hopeless.

Suppose you fill a car's gas tank to the brim with gasoline. Even if you were to poke a tiny hole in the tank, there would still be plenty of fuel to power the car at top speed. The only way anyone could really stop you would be to blast a major hole through the tank. That would certainly slow down the car—but it would also make it completely undriveable.

It works the same way with liquidity in the economy. A central bank can try to drain money out of the system, by raising interest rates, for example. But unless it takes drastic action—implementing truly deflationary policies like huge interest rate hikes—its efforts will be equivalent to that of a pinprick to the economy's gas tank. It will take many pinpricks and a long time to slow down the economic car.

In 1920s Germany, even if the central bank had tightened rather than loosened credit, it could not have averted the inflation to come. Similarly, the most our Federal Reserve bank will be able to do in the latter 1990s will be to pinprick the economy's gas tank.

The only way the Fed could really slow things down would be to make a move like the one Germany made following its inflation crisis, or as former Fed chairman Paul Volcker did in the late 1970s and early 1980s. A deflationary strategy would dramatically suck out the economy's liquidity. However, any action of this magnitude would also throw millions of people out of work and lead to the shutdown of whole industries. To take such a step would require an overwhelming political mandate along the lines of Paul Volcker's anti-inflation battle of 1979–1982, which landed the economy in its worst recession since the Great Depression of the 1930s.

That kind of iron political will (or, some would say, sadism) is clearly not present today in any of the world's capitals. In fact, the world is crying out for faster, not slower, economic growth—and inflation be damned! Considering the number of former incumbent politicians now out of a job, those remaining are unlikely to allow even supposedly "independent" central bankers that kind of latitude.

Consequently, the most we can expect the Fed to do is to keep poking tiny holes in the economy's tank. Enough fuel for ultrahigh inflation will remain.

Back to the 1970s

There is a very recent American example of a large monetary over-hang leading to rapid inflation. Take another look at the graph labeled "P/E Ratio S&P 400."

During the 1960s, stock market P/Es soared to levels almost as high as today's. As is the case today, stocks were at the end of a very long-lived bull market. Like now, investors were convinced that the markets were very low-risk ways to get rich, and were plowing record amounts of money into stocks.

Just as in the latter 1990s, there was a lot of money floating around the American economy during the latter 1960s. The Vietnam war was in full swing, as was the government's war on poverty. That had pushed up the level of government expenditures sharply. At the same time, Federal Reserve chairman Arthur Burns was responding to the economy's rapidly growing debt load by pump-ing up the growth of the money supply.

The high stock market valuations of that period were a direct result of the huge amount of money in the system. Once commodity prices started ticking up, inflationary expectations rose. That ignited the liquidity in the system, creating an inflationary explo-sion that was to rage unabated until 1980.

Today's levels of liquidity are even higher than those of the

1960s. It's still unlikely that the situation will get as far out of hand as in Germany after World War I, where the causes of inflation were far more numerous and complex. But today's high total debt and soaring stock prices certainly add up to enough monetary overhang for inflation to meet and beat what happened during the 1970s.

When monetary overhang reaches sky-high levels, it must be reduced somehow. The most painless way is inflation. That's because it's the easiest way to drive down the value of debt and bail out consumers.

One way to view total debt is as a bet on future growth. The higher the debt load, the greater the bet. Think of your own finances. The more money you borrow, the more dependent you are on future gains in income to pay off the debt. It works the same way for the economy. When debt is high, there must be tremendous growth to pay it off or massive bankruptcies will result.

High inflation is an easier way for governments to relieve a debt burden. If inflation is running at 10 percent a year, for example, a $100 debt will only be worth $90 a year later. That's another reason it will be very politically popular in coming years.

There is another possible outcome of today's monetary overhang problem: depression. Only once in the twentieth century has America's total monetary overhang been as high as it is today: during the Great Depression of the 1930s. That time, the government refused to inflate. The result was a massive wave of bankruptcies and human misery on a gigantic scale. The politicians who held the line on inflation, like President Herbert Hoover, were hung out to dry.

Prior to the Great Depression of the 1930s, the theories of John Maynard Keynes that governments could expand and contract economic growth were largely unknown and untested. Those who ran monetary policy simply didn't know that aggressive economic stimulation could save the day. In fact, the lesson of the German hyperinflation of the early 1920s was fresh in their minds. Most central bankers were determined not to take a chance on letting it happen in their countries.

The lesson of the 1930s is that aggressive stimulation can stem the tide of economic collapse and prevent a debt overhang avalanche. Economic policymakers ever since have followed the lesson diligently. Current Federal Reserve chairman, Alan Greenspan, for example, headed off collapse following the market crash of 1987 as well as during the recession of 1990.

Hopefully the lessons of the 1930s will also be followed by future policymakers in coming years, and we'll head off any future depression. Economic stimulation will have the powerful side effect of higher inflation. But no matter what happens, it couldn't be worse than a full-scale depression.

Three Building Blocks

And there you have it, the three building blocks that will bring on the coming inflation of the latter 1990s:

- The cry for growth from the growing American underclass, whose living standards will continue to fall due to foreign competition, downsizing-based productivity gains and lack of educational opportunity.
- The bull market in basic commodities, fueled by explosive demand from the developing world.
- The huge monetary/debt overhang, which will be soaked up only by rising inflation.

As we approach the new millennium, both the service sector and the manufacturing sector of the American economy will face rising competition from overseas. In manufacturing, that will force companies to boost productivity in ways that hurt rather than help workers, such as layoffs. The same thing will happen to most service sector workers.

The only exceptions will be the fortunate few whose skills, experience and education become indispensible to their companies—the knowledge worker elite. But most people's buying power will stay in the now generation-long downtrend, widening social and economic inequalities to dangerous levels. The result will be a deafening cry for faster economic growth to ease the pain, echoed around the world. Shell-shocked politicians will rush to obey.

As growth is pumped up, demand for basic commodities in the developed world will increase. In the world's high-growth, less-developed nations like China and India, it will explode. Coupled with today's low supply levels, that will send prices of all commodities soaring. Price increases could get very steep if problems arise in some of the world's more unstable producing nations, or if producers decide to price their raw materials in another currency besides the U.S. dollar. Rising commodity prices will flow right into higher prices for all other goods and services—and higher inflation.

Once inflation does start to spark up, the huge liquidity over-hang will catch fire. This, in turn, will trigger rising inflationary expectations, which will beget ever-higher rates of inflation, as companies, individuals and governments struggle to keep their heads above water.

It's not a pretty picture. But it's one that will be with us into the next century. The only real question now is how long it will take for this to happen. Unfortunately, the answer is sooner than you think. In fact, the real watershed event to usher in this volatile new era may have already occurred. In part two of this book, we outline an investment roadmap for the decade ahead.

Investment Roadmap
for a Rocky Road

6

Investing in a Volatile Decade

Most of us take for granted that the future will look about like the present. Few on either Wall Street or Main Street expect anything like the future we've painted here. Instead, most people look for continued low inflation, steady economic growth and higher stock and bond prices.

At the moment, they appear to be right, at least on paper. Here in the mid-1990s, the economy is growing steadily, unemployment is near its lowest rate in decades and inflation seems well-behaved. American technology is leading the world and creating a new sense of optimism for the future. In short, the economic and market conditions of the 1980s and early 1990s are still very much with us.

Just as it's hard to imagine a winter snowstorm on a blisteringly hot summer day, it's tough now to picture hard times for the economy and the markets. But just as surely they will come, and a lot sooner than almost anyone expects.

Every quantum shift in the economy and financial markets has first encountered such disbelief. In the early stages, Wall Street and Main Street simply ignore the changes. Later, as evidence builds and more things that once seemed permanent start to change form, they practice denial. Only when the trend has been in motion for a while and is nearing an end will it become universally recognized enough for everyone to feel comfortable about it.

The key to long-term trends in the financial markets is inflation. Its actual level, whether it's rising or falling, what the outlook for it is—these are the questions that shape the future of the economy and markets for everything from stocks to real estate.

From the early 1980s up until recently, the financial markets climbed a wall of worry about inflation. With the rapid inflation of the 1970s fresh in mind, the average investor was very cautious about entering the market. Any hint that inflation was coming back would send most people scurrying for the exits.

Today, the low inflation trend has gone on for so long that even novices have lost their fear. True to form, they've begun pouring into stocks precisely when the long-term trend in inflation is about to shift upward.

Rapid inflation will come as a colossal shock to most investors, brokers and Wall Street analysts. Americans in the mid-1990s are deeply imbued with the idea that steady buying of stocks, bonds and mutual funds is a sure-fire way to build a fortune. In fact, making big money fast in stocks and bonds is widely perceived today as an entitlement, rather than the result of hard work or even good luck.

The rules of the game for the next ten years will be markedly different. The experience of the last high-inflation period—from 1965 through 1981—provides a clue to what we can expect.

Over that time, the Dow Industrials failed to make a single new all-time high. Even the best stocks weren't immune to the malaise of that now-forgotten era. Rising inflation and uneven economic growth periodically wreaked havoc on the stock and bond markets, subjecting both to terrifying bear markets interspersed with uneven rallies.

A complacent buy-and-hold strategy for stocks, bonds and diversified mutual funds—the same approach that later worked so well in the 1980s—was a complete disaster during the 1970s. The bright side of that decade was that "real" assets, such as precious metals, real estate and energy, made many people rich. In fact, the opportunities to get rich in the 1970s were much greater than those during the bull market days of the 1980s.

The key to profiting in any new era is recognizing that the ground is shifting and changing your strategy accordingly. The time for such action is now.

The first part of this book identified the three building blocks of the coming inflation—the cry for growth, the commodities bull market and the monetary/debt overhang. These are already well in place, and are gaining strength. In fact, the key watershed event to herald the coming of the new era of high inflation has already occurred. Now let's look at the best places to put your money.

Shifting Ground

In mid-October 1993, thirty-year Treasury bond yields touched below 5.75 percent for the first time since the early 1970s—before the Arab oil shocks created the country's first post–World War II inflationary spiral.

Bonds had averaged unprecedented yearly returns of 10 to 15 percent since the early 1980s, as inflation fell from double-digit levels to a well-behaved 2 to 3 percent. Many forecasted that yields would continue falling to the 3 percent range. Few could conceive that the good times might be coming to an end, but they were.

They had no way of knowing it at the time, but giddy traders were buying bonds hand over fist at what was almost certainly the peak of the fifteen-year bull market for bonds that began in the early 1980s. In the months that followed, bond prices plunged sharply. Yields ultimately hit a short-term peak in the 8 percent area, translating into losses of 20 to 25 percent in just a few short months.

In 1995, bonds rode a crest of optimism that the newly elected Republican Congress would soon balance the federal budget. Bond yields, however, fell only as far as the 6 percent range. And by early 1996, the pro-growth rhetoric of upcoming national elections had ruined this mood, sending bond prices down again to prices well below the records set in October 1993. Bonds' 1993 peak and subsequent reversal is clear evidence that the tide has turned for inflation.

The last quantum shift in the economy and markets—which heralded an era of low inflation and the rise of the 1980s bull market in stocks and bonds—was the early 1980 collapse of gold prices from their peak.

As 1980 opened, rampant inflation was arguably more of a problem than it had ever been in American history. In January 1980, the year-over-year change in producer prices was close to 15 percent, while consumer prices were increasing by nearly 1 percent a month.

Prices of real assets like gold were soaring. From its low of around $100 an ounce in 1976, the yellow metal had risen to an all-time high of more than $800 in barely four years. Rising real estate prices made scores of American home owners wealthy. Energy prices soared as the world got drunk on ever-larger amounts of OPEC oil. Stocks and bonds were in the doghouse.

Then suddenly, almost inexplicably, gold prices collapsed. From January to March 1980, the yellow metal tumbled more than 25 percent from its January high. It never again came close to that lofty height.

Few recognized it at the time, but gold's move was a clear sign that a new day of lower inflation and more stable economic growth was dawning. Federal Reserve chairman Paul Volcker represented a reborn political will to fight inflation after the catastrophic 1970s, a mind-set that remained in place between then and now.

In other markets, the reaction time was considerably slower. AAA corporate bonds, for example, didn't reach peak yields of around 16 percent until September 1981. The stock market didn't bottom until August 1982 with the Dow Jones Industrial Average in the 780 range, more than 20 percent below its highs of the mid-1960s. Until those markets turned around—confirming the switch to low inflation—gold's drop was considered a fluke.

The market and economic situation in mid-1995 is a mirror image of the one in 1980. The only difference is that we're heralding an era of higher, not lower, inflation.

Now as then, the major watershed event—a sudden 25 percent drop in bond prices from late 1993 through early 1994—has been shrugged off as a nonevent. And just as gold's horrific drop in 1980 looked completely out of place in an environment of rising inflation, so bonds' big bust looks at odds with today's low inflation.

The other major markets continue to live in a dreamworld of low inflation, with stocks making new highs and real assets like gold languishing. And bonds' stunning drop in 1994 followed by a partial recovery in 1995 matches the action in gold from 1980 to 1981.

History never repeats itself exactly. And it will take a long time for the reversal in inflation to be fully felt both in the markets and in the financial economy. Most investors wrongly reasoned after gold fell in 1980 that precious metals were still the place to be and that stocks and bonds were to be avoided. After bonds' 1995 recovery sent stocks to a record year, most today insist that stocks and bonds are still the ticket to riches, despite bonds' inability to hit new highs. Unfortunately, today's bond buyers will get as badly burned as their "goldbug" forebears were in the early 1980s, when the inflation trend shifted down.

Regardless of how it plays out exactly, the factors leading inflation lower for more than a decade have now clearly run their course. More important, the three building blocks—the cry for growth, rising commodity prices, and monetary and debt overhang—that will lead inflation higher have just begun to be felt. Just as the age of real assets ended in January 1980, the age of buy and hold for financial assets probably came to an end in October 1993.

Real Assets Rise, Financial Assets Fall

Over the long haul, inflation is the prime mover of investment markets. When it's falling, financial assets like stocks and bonds thrive. When it's rising, real assets like gold, oil and real estate take over.

From the early 1980s through the mid-1990s, inflation has been generally well-behaved. As a result, stocks and bonds have soared. As values have gone nowhere but up, making money on Wall Street has demanded about as much acuity as operating an electric pencil sharpener.

In contrast, the decade ahead will be burdened by rising inflation. As in the 1970s, most stocks and bonds will lose ground. You'll once again have to earn the money you make in the markets with honest hard work. Simply buying and holding any stocks, bonds and diversified mutual funds will be a formula for disaster.

It's indisputable that stocks and bonds have made money over the very long term. Unfortunately, there have been plenty of uncomfortably long periods when it has paid to be on the sidelines. Those who bought at the top in 1929, for example, needed more than a generation just to make back what they lost to the Great Crash. The latter 1990s will be such a time as well.

Throughout the 1980s and early 1990s, central banks focused on fighting inflation. Wall Street prospered under low inflation and stable economic growth. In contrast, the 1970s were a time of rapid inflation and uneven growth, disastrous for stocks and bonds. Inflation ahead means the latter 1990s will likely be a repeat of the 1970s.

What will be the investments of choice in the years ahead? Our table labeled "Annual Rates of Return" is the best possible roadmap available. It shows how various investments—from stocks to gold—have historically performed at different levels of inflation.

The last period of sustained high inflation the world faced was

ANNUAL RATES OF RETURN						
	CPI	Stocks	Bonds	Housing	Farmland	Silver
Deflation						
1929-32	-6.4%	-21.2%	5.0%	-3.9%	-12.3%	-19.8%
Stable Prices						
1921-29	-1.3	20.2	6.4	5.4	-2.8	-3.3
1934-40	1.0	12.2	6.2	0.7	3.9	1.0
Average	-0.2	16.2	6.3	3.1	0.6	1.2
Declining & Moderate Inflation						
1942-45	2.5	26.1	4.5	10.0	18.1	-3.3
1949-65	2.1	17.5	2.0	6.1	8.6	5.2
1981-84	3.9	16.8	20.0	3.6-	-2.4	13.1
1985-90	3.5	20.3	14.5	-	-	5.5
Average	3.0	20.2	10.3	6.6	8.1	5.7
Rapid Inflation						
1940-47	6.8	12.3	2.6	12.2	18.5	8.6
1965-81	7.1	6.4	6.1	10.3	12.7	23.7
Average	7.0	9.4	4.4	11.3	15.6	16.2

Source: Morgan Stanley and *Investment Strategist*

from 1965 through 1981. Investments that did well then should do well in the next ten to fifteen years. From our table, precious metals (represented by silver since gold prices were only decontrolled in the early 1970s) were far and away the best place to put your money, rising 23.7 percent annually for the period.

Real assets do well in times of rising inflation. That's because uncertainty is king and long-term planning is almost pointless. Investors are only willing to hold assets that will keep their value as paper money loses its allure. They will pay up for real, tangible assets like commodities and real estate.

As our table makes clear, the 1965–1981 period was obviously not the best of times for stocks and bonds. Both of these financial assets netted negative real (inflation-adjusted) returns for the entire sixteen years. That's a long time to be under water.

The results were markedly worse for the 1966–1974 period. That was nearly an entire decade in which most stocks did not even generate positive nominal returns.

Moreover, there was also a big price to pay for standing still: the gut-wrenching volatility of the period, including the huge sell-off of 1973/74, when many large blue-chip stocks lost more than half their value in a devastating decline.

Bonds were certainly no picnic either. Top-quality bond yields rose from the 4 to 5 percent range in the mid-1960s to a high of over 15 percent in the early 1980s. Bondholders who hung on until their bonds matured of course received their full principal, but suffered an enormous loss of purchasing power. Clearly the road to riches in a world of rapidly rising inflation does not run through financial assets such as stocks and bonds.

A Roadmap for the 1990s

Poor returns for stocks as a group don't mean every stock will flounder. Neither do they spell curtains for every fixed-income investment. We're convinced that if you work hard you will be able to find companies that will score great gains in an otherwise desultory financial environment.

Also, not every real asset will be a guaranteed winner for the long term. There will be plenty of ways to lose money in bad real estate, gold coin and collectibles scams or bad energy stocks.

The tough years ahead will be a time of staggering opportunities for those who recognize them. Higher inflation does not necessarily mean economic catastrophe. In fact, it's quite the opposite.

The low inflation of the 1980s and early 1990s came at the price of historically slow economic growth. That below-average growth accelerated the prolonged downtrend in Americans' real, or inflation-adjusted, wages. One of the positive things about the latter 1990s will be at least a temporary reversal of this trend.

Just like during the 1980s, there will be plenty of opportunities to score massive investment profits. The difference is that financial markets in the latter 1990s are going to be much more volatile. Timing will become far more essential to success. Hard assets like real estate and gold will trade places with financial assets as the portfolio picks of choice. It will still be an age of opportunity—but the opportunities will be considerably different from those of the 1980s.

The rest of this book focuses on each of these opportunities and how nimble investors can capitalize on the new environment.

7

Stocks: How to Beat the Wall Street Bear

During the bull market of the last fifteen years, you didn't have to be a genius to make money in stocks—just patient enough to wait for the inevitable upswing.

Unfortunately, the next fifteen years won't be nearly so easy. You'll not only have to pick the right stocks, you'll have to time your entry and exit points well to avoid the inevitable crushing sell-offs.

High and rising inflation will take the stock market on quite a roller-coaster ride in coming years. Fortunately, there's a relatively easy way to make sure you get in at the bottoms and out at the tops: Buy when inflationary pressures are receding, and sell when they begin to grow again.

Two Bulls and a Bear

In the short run, everything from Federal Reserve chairman Alan Greenspan's statements to mundane economic statistics can send stocks soaring or crashing. Long-term, only inflation holds sway on Wall Street.

When inflation is low and falling, stocks prosper. When inflation is high and rising, stocks just can't keep up. Buy and hold is a disaster.

Inflation is so important because stocks live and die on the prospects for noninflationary economic growth. Noninflationary growth is only possible when inflation is low.

Over the long term, the stock market can be thought of as a weighing machine. The companies with the most "meat," or earnings growth, wind up with the highest prices. The focus is on the future—no one cares about last year's results. Basically, if current profit growth rates can be sustained or increased, people are willing to pay more for stocks.

For the overall stock market, economic growth sets the tone for earnings growth. Stocks as a group "weigh" most when current growth is slow and has plenty of room to rise without igniting inflation. Stocks "weigh" least when inflation is rising and there's little room for faster noninflationary growth.

The best proof of inflation's impact is the history of the stock market since World War II. Take a look at the table labeled "Inflation and Stock Returns," which shows the performance of the S&P 400 industrial stocks in that time frame.

U.S. stock prices are considerably higher now than they were when the Japanese surrendered back in 1945. Obviously, a buy-and-hold strategy over that entire period would have been wildly profitable. But look a bit more closely at the table. Stocks'

INFLATION AND STOCK RETURNS			
	1948–65	1966–81	1982–95
Inflation	1.7%	7.0%	3.6%
Stock Returns	16.3	5.9%	15.9%

actual performance can be divided into three periods: two bullish, one bearish.

From 1948 through 1965, the market was on a tear, rising 16.3 percent a year on average. Then, starting in 1966, things changed for the worse. Stocks ran in place for a few years before the bottom dropped out with the Great Bear Market of 1973/74. The market was then flat until about 1982, at which time the third period—the bull market of the 1980s and early 1990s—was launched.

Stocks were a great place to be during the first period, from 1948 through 1965. They were a horrible investment in the second, which lasted from 1966 into 1981. They've been a great bet in the fifteen years since.

Buying and holding over the past fifty years was a winning strategy. But you would have done far better had you hedged your bets a bit during the bear market in between.

What did the two bull markets have in common that the bear period did not share? Not politics. The latter 1960s and '70s were a turbulent time for American society, while the 1950s and 1980s were relatively calm. There were both Democratic and Republican presidents for wide stretches during all three eras, and the Democrats controlled both houses of Congress most of the time as well.

Prosperity wasn't a common element either. The 1948–1965 bull period was a true golden age for the American economy. Rising productivity boosted incomes for both rich and poor.

In contrast, throughout the 1980s and '90s bull market, economic growth has remained relatively sluggish and unemployment high, productivity has stagnated, real incomes have fallen and inequalities between rich and poor have widened. Stocks soared and the rich got richer, but the poor and even the middle class have struggled.

You could even make the case that the 1966–1981 bear period had more in common with the first bull market. Economic life was much more tumultuous. But worker buying power still managed to increase for about half the period and the economy grew rapidly.

There's only one thing the two bull markets had in common that the bear market did not: low inflation. During the first bull market period, stock investors saw gains multiply at a 16.3 percent rate. At the same time, inflation, as measured by the CPI, averaged a scant 1.7 percent a year.

Similarly, inflation has been in a steep downtrend during the second bull market. From 1981, when it hit a peak in the high teens, CPI inflation has fallen to a well-behaved annual rate of 2 to 3 percent. During that time, the profits for stocks have been almost as good as in the first bull market. Nominal returns averaged nearly 16 percent a year, while inflation averaged 3.6 percent.

Inflation rose sharply during the bear market, averaging 7 percent a year for the period and hitting double digits for uncomfortably long periods of time. Stocks underwent dramatic ups and downs, but overall returns fell to less than 6 percent a year.

Clearly, inflation has set the stock market's long-term course more than any other factor. The easiest way to make money in the market long-term is to buy and hold when it's at bay, as it was during the two bull markets.

When the long-term trend in inflation is up, the example of the 1966 to 1981 period shows that you can still make money, if you time the ups and downs correctly. The key again is keeping an eye on inflation—buying on downticks and selling on upticks.

What Lies Ahead

If the experience of the 1970s is any guide, inflation, while in a dramatic long-term uptrend, will still ebb and flow several times over the next decade or so. Whenever it backs off, stocks will almost certainly rally strongly. Whenever it rises, stocks will tread water at best. Worst of all, when recessions occur, big bad bear markets will result.

For example, in the early 1970s, America was hit by a recession, which triggered a horrible two-year bear market. Major blue-chip companies lost almost half of their value during the period, and smaller shares did even worse.

The fortunate outcome of the period was that inflation was cooled off considerably. The six months following former President Richard Nixon's August 1974 resignation were extraordinarily good for stocks, with the average S&P 400 industrial stock soaring 30 percent. The major reason was that the economy was recovering from a recession. It had plenty of room to grow without igniting inflation.

The key to making money in stocks over the next decade or so will be the same as it has been throughout the post–World War II period. Mainly, buy when inflation is low and falling; sell or stand aside when it's high and rising. When the relentless upward push of inflation cools, stocks do best. When economic growth and inflation are reaccelerating, stocks and bonds fare poorly.

Unlike investors who bought at the tops in 1987 and 1990, you won't be bailed out from any errors you make, as they were. Those who bought at the beginning of the last high-inflation era in 1965— or immediately prior to the 1973/74 bear market—still haven't broken even, adjusted for inflation. Buy-and-holders in 1929 were in the red for more than a generation.

We can't stress this enough: If you're going to play with stocks in the latter 1990s, it's absolutely vital that you stay nimble. That means keeping your eye on inflation, buying when it backs off and being ready to cut and run when the economic forces inevitably bring it roaring back.

✳ One Simple Rule

Economists have immense models to forecast and gauge inflation. Fortunately, investors can get by with just one simple rule: Buy and hold stocks when the Producer Price Index (PPI) twelve-month rate of change is below 4.25 percent. Sell when the rate of change rises above 4.25 percent.

The CPI measures price changes for a basket of goods and services "typically" purchased by consumers. The PPI is closer to the root of inflation because it gauges price changes in materials used to make those goods and services—for example, machinery used in creating consumer goods. In other words, changes in the PPI foreshadow changes in the CPI, making it a better indicator of inflation.

As long as the PPI is well-behaved—and below 4.25 percent has historically qualified as such—inflation is not out of control. The current rate of economic growth, whatever it is, is sustainable. The economic train may be steaming down the track as it was during the 1950s and '60s, or it may be just barely chugging along as in the 1980s and early 1990s. Either way, the economic engine will be running cool. Businesses can plan on expanding, corporate earnings will rise and stock prices will soar.

The example of the past fifty years bears this out, as you can see in the table labeled "Buy Low, Sell High." If you had bought and held stocks only when the PPI was less than 4.25 percent—disregarding any other variable—your money would have compounded at an average annual rate of 15.5 percent. That's well above the market's average long-term return of around 9 percent.

The second half of our rule is to sell stocks when the PPI rises above 4.25 percent. The idea here is that when the PPI gets out of control, higher inflation can't be far behind.

BUY LOW, SELL HIGH	
Holding Period	**Total Return***
December 1951–December 1956	151.0%
February 1957–November 1969	231.0
May 1970–August 1972	56.0
December 1975–January 1976	12.0
September 1976–December 1976	3.0
March 1982–August 1987	268.0
January 1988–July 1988	8.0
August 1988–December 1988	7.0
August 1989–October 1990	-10.0
January 1991–May 1995	76.0
Average Annual Compound Return	15.49%

*Returns for buying S&P 400 index when PPI has fallen below 4.25%, holding until PPI rises above 4.25% since December 1951.

For the past fifteen years, the Federal Reserve has been willing to cool off too-hot economic growth. As the 1990s progress, the political will for such action will almost certainly fade, given the drop in real incomes over the past twenty years. But sustainable economic growth will be practically impossible. Businesses will not be able to plan far ahead, earnings will stagnate and possibly lose ground to inflation, and stocks will languish at best, plummet at worst.

If you had bought and held stocks during all the periods when the PPI was above 4.25 percent since World War II, your average annual total return would have been just 1.8 percent. Excluding dividends, you would have lost money. Including inflation, you would have lost some bigtime money.

To capture even that paltry return, you would have had to hang on through some of the most gut-wrenching bear markets of this century. Some examples: the 1969/70 decline, the massive sell-off of 1973/74 and the autumn crash of 1987. Clearly, it has paid to follow our simple rule to the letter, whether the market's long-term trend has been up or down.

Unlike during the two post–World War II bull markets, sell signals are certain to be triggered more frequently in the latter 1990s, as they were during the inflationary 1970s. PPI growth moved above 4.25 percent just once during the first bull market, and four times during the most recent one. That left huge stretches when no signals were reported, such as from March 1982 through August 1987. Inflation was at bay throughout.

During the inflationary 1970s, in contrast, PPI growth was above 4.25 percent most of the time. There were just three different buy signals, and each was short-lived. To sell was the prudent course most of the time.

America's root economic problems today are much worse than during the 1970s. That means more volatility and inflation lie ahead. It will be even more imperative to keep up with this vital indicator.

PPI figures are reported in almost any financial publication, on most news broadcasts and in most daily newspapers. They're announced monthly by the U.S. Department of Labor.

What to Buy

When the PPI says it's time to buy, what stocks should you choose? We've based all of our calculations on the performance of a very broad-based market average, the S&P 400 index of the largest U.S. industrial companies. Together, these 400 stocks represent most of the market's typical volume, making them a good proxy for the average stock.

Obviously, some stocks will radically outperform the averages in the years ahead, such as the energy, small stocks and gold stocks we recommend in later chapters. Some will dramatically under-perform. To take full advantage of our system, however, you don't have to be a stock picker. You just have to make sure your portfolio reflects what's going to happen in the market averages—the Dow Jones and the S&P. That means diversification.

How you diversify is largely a matter of personal preference, as well as the size of your wallet. The easiest way is through big stock mutual funds. Mutual funds are managed professionally, so you'll avoid most of the worst mistakes of individual stock investing. They also allow you to own a broad-based portfolio for a relatively low initial investment, typically $1,000 to $3,000.

Since the key here is to at least match the big stock averages when there is a green light, one fund that comes immediately to mind is the **Vanguard Index 500 Fund** (800-662-7447). By construc-tion this fund matches the Standard & Poor index of the 500 largest U.S. stocks. If you buy the fund when inflation ticks below 4.25 per-cent and switch out of it when inflation moves above that, you'll be a happy camper.

It may be possible to do better than an index fund, if you pick your funds wisely. The three big cap funds listed in our table have outperformed the market averages over the long pull. They're no-load funds—they charge no fees to either buy or sell shares—and have experienced managers who have beaten the averages in both bull and bear markets. Any of these will do.

These are by no means the only funds out there worth looking

FUNDS FOR PLAYING RALLIES

Fund (phone)	
Columbia Growth Fund (800-547-1707)	Management team picks variety of growth-oriented stocks.
Fidelity Magellan (800-544-8888)	Huge fund can move market on its own. Great in rallies, but a bear market disaster
Janus Fund (800-525-8983)	Well-run fund with focus on strong companies and does some market timing.
Scudder Growth and Income (800-225-2470)	A more conservative way to play rallies, probably with less risk.

at. Many of those you already own will do quite nicely. Just make sure they meet the following handful of criteria:

• *Funds must be no-load (i.e., impose no sales charges or redemption fees).* There are some great stock funds that do charge a fee for new investments. However, there are just as many great funds that don't. In a market where extreme volatility spells the death of buy and hold as a viable investment strategy, you'll need maximum flexibility to move in and out of your fund.

Funds that impose withdrawal penalties or that bill you for moving back in will make it too tempting to just hang in there and hope for the best. That could be a mistake it will take years to recover from. Do yourself a favor, stick with no-loads.

• *Funds should beat the S&P 400 industrials index in both bull and bear markets.* A rising tide raises all ships, and a falling tide will lower them. But if a fund has beaten the major averages in both up and down markets over the long pull, managers have shown they have the knack for picking good stocks over a multi-year period.

• *Funds should be adequately diversified and not overly volatile.* One often overlooked sin is having a fund overly committed to just a few stocks or a particular sector. This leaves it open to problems with those shares. To find out if a fund is overdoing it, check its "r2" (R-squared), a statistical measure of correlation between a fund and the S&P 500. The closer a fund's r2 approaches that of the S&P 400, which is 100, the more diversified it is and the less vulnerable it is to disaster in a single stock. Generally, r2s of 70 or higher are diversified enough. The most complete source for r2s is Chicago-based *Morningstar Mutual Funds* (800-876-5005). It's found in many libraries. The persistent can often find r2s by phoning the funds themselves.

• *Funds should have had the same manager for at least three years.* A fund's success or failure depends almost entirely on the skill of its manager or managers. If a fund has switched managers or has a history of doing so, there are no guarantees the new hand at the wheel will drive as smoothly.

Notable exceptions are funds that are managed by a group of advisors. These funds are governed more by a set strategy and philosophy, rather than the instincts and skills of a single manager.

Just as with top-quality individual stocks, great funds can lose their way. To ensure you're getting the most for your money, you'll have to run your selections periodically through the vigorous criteria listed above. Also, other great funds may emerge that you won't want to miss out on, so a periodic check of other selections won't hurt.

If you choose funds that meet these criteria, you'll make the most of the infrequent but rewarding stock market booms of the next fifteen years. The few minutes of your time that you spend checking them out will pay rich dividends for years to come.

No-load funds will be easy to cash out of when the PPI generates a sell signal (i.e., rises above 4.25 percent), since you pay no sales commissions or exit fees. In contrast, a diversified portfolio of individual blue-chip stocks (ten to twelve companies) or a loaded fund will cost you money every time you cash out or buy back in. Given the number of times buy-and-sell signals could be generated in the volatile times ahead, that could get quite expensive.

If you follow our simple rules carefully, the gains you reap from even the most ordinary no-load stock fund could easily exceed what traders made in the buy-and-hold 1980s and early 1990s. But let the buyer beware: The buy-and-hold days are over. Getting out at the right time is just as important as getting in. Navigating the stock market's treacherous waters in coming years will depend on skillful timing, and that means keeping your eyes and ears open for inflation!

8

Small Stocks for the Next Century

Ever dreamed of buying the next Microsoft or Wal-Mart? Your chances will never be better than during the next ten years.

The rapid economic growth and high inflation of the latter 1990s and early twenty-first century will ease the creation of hundreds of new businesses. Those that strike it big will reward their investors by multiplying their money many times.

Your odds of landing the next Microsoft are not incredibly great. But in the faster-growth, higher-inflation latter 1990s, even the average small stock will leave the big boys in the dust. In fact, small stocks have historically been one of the very best ways to beat rapid inflation.

During the 1966–1981 bear market, the smallest one-fifth of New York Stock Exchange stocks averaged a gain of more than 14 percent a year. That was more than twice both the rate of inflation and the average annual return on the typical big stock.

Some small stocks did spectacularly better. By 1980, for example, computer chip company Intel's stock price was forty times higher than it had been in 1973. Early buyers of Digital Equipment paid about $7 per share in 1966. By 1980, the stock sold for about $300, taking splits into account.

Unlike the larger stocks that make up the major averages, small stocks thrive when inflation is on the move. It's much easier to grow when prices are rising and the economy is booming. It's also much easier for a company with $1 million in sales to double its revenue than it is for a $1 billion outfit to do the same. When growth is booming, therefore, small companies' growth rates are generally much higher than those of larger companies. Higher inflation puts a premium on growth, so small stocks are the market's top performers.

Conversely, when growth is sluggish, it's easier for the big boys to control the marketplace. Small stocks lag behind. For much of the 1980s and early 1990s, that's exactly what happened. Generally slow economic growth and low inflation put the big stocks at the top of the heap. Small stocks fell back. From January 1983 through December 1990, the smallest one-fifth of New York Stock Exchange stocks averaged a gain of just 2.6 percent a year. In contrast, the big S&P 400 stock average gained 14.6 percent annually.

The 1970s weren't all gravy for the half-pints. During the recessionary sell-off of 1972–1974, the average small stock lost over 50 percent of its value. That was actually a good deal worse than the performance of the big stock averages. Small stocks lose more in downturns because little companies' very lives are often at stake when growth slows down. In fact, the average small stock is among the very worst investments you can hold during a recession.

The high inflation and jagged economic growth of the latter 1990s and early twenty-first century will almost certainly be interspersed with crippling recessions. That will subject small fry to devastating bear markets. When they occur, you'll want to be miles away from small stocks.

But if you can avoid the occasional blasts from the bear, small stocks' ability to thrive in inflationary times will make them an overall bright spot in your portfolio. Even if your picks don't become the next Intels, you'll still reap big profits. If you're lucky, the sky's the limit.

The Power of Growth

The key to avoiding recessionary blowouts with small stocks is understanding what makes small stocks thrive when inflation is high.

Since the mid-1920s, as far back as records are available, the small-est 20 percent of New York Stock Exchange stocks have chalked up an average annual return of 12.2 percent. Large stocks, as measured by the S&P 400 industrials, averaged only 10.2 percent.

As our table shows, small stocks have done much better when inflation has been on the move. Since 1926, whenever the CPI rose over a five-year period, small stocks led the way. And when the CPI was rising at a 5 percent clip or higher, the tally was small stocks 21.2 percent a year and big stocks just 9.4 percent. CPI growth of over 7 percent widened the gap even more, with small stocks post-ing gains three times larger than the big boys.

INFLATION IS THE KEY			
	Small Stocks	Large Stocks	Difference
Falling Inflation	8.4%	11.9%	-3.5%
Rising Inflation*	17.7	8.8	+8.9
Rising High Inflation†	21.2	9.4	+11.8
Rising Very High Inflation‡	26.2	9.6	+16.6

Average annual rate of return (5-year periods).
*Rising = 5-year CPI (CPI average is above 10-year CPI average); †High = 5-year CPI is greater than 5 percent; ‡Very High = 5-year CPI is greater than 7 percent.

Why do small stocks do so well in times of rising inflation? Sim-ply because on average they have more growth potential and entail more risk than big stocks. They perform best when investors are focusing more on growth and less on risk.

When economic growth is blasting ahead, inflation is typically rising. Investors' paramount concern at such times will be keeping up with inflation. Small stocks' earnings can grow much faster when inflation is high and rising than they can when it's low or falling. For one thing, faster inflation causes market conditions to be less competitive. Protecting and gaining market share is less impor-tant than generating higher sales. There's enough to go around for both the small and large to profit.

When competition isn't so intense, it's far easier for a $100 million company to double its revenue than it is for a multibillion-dollar com-pany to do so. In other words, even if they don't take market share from the big boys, small fry will add sales. And the smaller they are, the less of an increase it will take to generate a higher percentage gain.

Small stocks' close relationship with inflation makes them a great inflation hedge. In fact, history shows that, except when inflation is really flying, they've done a better job than gold, the quintessential inflation hedge.

The price of gold was not deregulated until the early 1970s, when then-President Nixon took the world off the gold standard. Consequently, we only have records for free market gold prices for the past twenty years or so. But since the early 1970s, whenever CPI inflation has been at least 7 percent and rising, gold and other precious metals have averaged a return of about 16 percent per year. That's far less than small stocks' average annual 21.2 percent gain during that same period.

Knowing the Danger Signs

Unfortunately, the figures showing small stocks' long-term superiority over large shares also mask one other fact: During times of slow growth and moderate inflation, investors are more focused on safety and opt for the more reliable earnings growth of big companies. As a result, small stocks underperform.

When inflation is falling and economic growth is slow, competition intensifies for ever-smaller markets. Companies focus more on increasing their share of the shrinking marketplace than on boosting sales from new sources. Big companies' entrenched market positions and larger bank accounts give them a huge advantage. They can absorb economic shocks more easily, and they can reduce prices with less hardship, to cut out competition.

Unless their products have a clearly defined and growing niche, small companies can be cut out of the picture during recessions, as the big boys drive to increase sales by expanding market share. Even if they do have a niche, they could suffer should customers consider their products nonessential. In a slow-growth economy, it's tough for small companies to grow.

Our first table, labeled "Inflation Is the Key," shows how small stocks fare poorly in slow-growth environments. Whenever inflation has been falling, small stocks have underperformed large ones. During full-fledged recessions, the gap has widened even more. For example during the 1972–1974 sell-off, big stocks lost an average of 35 percent, as measured by the S&P 400 Industrial Average.

That was bad. But far worse was the catastrophic near–50 percent loss suffered by the smallest one-fifth of the New York Stock Exchange between February 1972 and December 1974. Many small companies went belly-up during those years. And some broad averages of very small stocks lost 90 percent of their value.

Much higher inflation in the years ahead is extremely bullish for small stocks, whose profits will probably be greatest as the economy soars toward its peaks. Unfortunately, the inevitable valleys we hit will almost certainly wipe out all but the heartiest fry, just as they've done in past inflationary periods. Timing small stocks is even more important than with bigger stocks.

We have two simple rules for reaping the profits and avoiding the pitfalls: Buy small stocks whenever the annual rate of growth in the CPI rises above 7 percent. Sell small stocks or stand aside when the CPI's growth rate falls below 4.5 percent. (And, of course, as we indicated in the last chapter, switch into big stocks when the PPI drops below 4.25 percent.)

Following these rules is a proven formula for success in inflationary times. In April 1973, CPI growth moved above 7 percent, triggering our buy signal. It stayed above 5 percent for nearly a decade, until November 1982. During that period, the average small stock scored almost a sevenfold advance. The average annualized gain of 22.6 percent is among the highest long-term returns for any investment ever. That's in sharp contrast to the flat returns on big stocks. The graph labeled "Rule #1 for Small Stock Shoppers" demonstrates the success of our rule.

Perhaps the most remarkable period was between mid-1976 and mid-1982. During those six years the Dow fell from about 1000 to

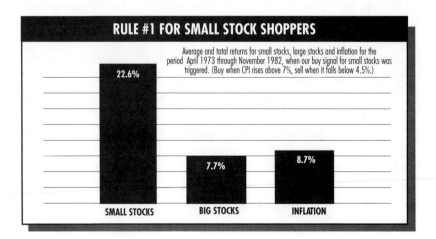

RULE #1 FOR SMALL STOCK SHOPPERS

Average and total returns for small stocks, large stocks and inflation for the period April 1973 through November 1982, when our buy signal for small stocks was triggered. (Buy when CPI rises above 7%, sell when it falls below 4.5%.)

22.6%

7.7%

8.7%

SMALL STOCKS   BIG STOCKS   INFLATION

780. As a result, it was a period largely regarded as terrible for stocks, especially with inflation averaging over 9 percent a year. Not so for investors who focused on small stocks. During those six years the average small stock (i.e., the smallest 20 percent of New York Stock Exchange shares) returned an average of over 24 percent a year. Had you bought the typical small fry, you would have nearly quadrupled your money during those six years.

When inflation is rising, your portfolio should be weighted toward small stocks. When it's low and falling, big ones are the best bets.

There will be times when inflation is rising so fast that it must be slowed down. When the Federal Reserve is forced to put its foot on the brake to prevent a hyperinflationary financial meltdown, small stocks will be among the worst possible investments you can own. You'll want to be long gone.

That's why we've added one additional rule for investing in small stocks: Sell if the annualized growth rate of the PPI rises above 15 percent. Should PPI inflation reach that neighborhood, the Fed will be forced to take some drastic deflationary action. As it slams on the brakes, a recession will be unavoidable. A harsh bear market for small stocks will follow.

As long as inflation remains in a long-term uptrend, small stocks will outperform big ones mightily when the market recovers. So once stocks do hit bottom, you'll want to load up on small stocks, not big ones.

Small Stock Shopping

There are two ways to go about investing in small stocks. You can try to pick out your own "next Wal-Marts." Or, you can let a seasoned fund manager do it for you.

For those with less deep pockets, small stock mutual funds are the way to play. For best results, use the same selection criteria as for big stock funds, except for the "r2" rule. Small stocks and funds are by nature more volatile than the S&P 500, so this criterion is best ignored when choosing them. One excellent choice is **Barron Asset Management** (800-992-2766).

If you go the individual stock route, wise selection is crucial. Some small fry are headed for stardom. Others may not be in business in two years, especially if they rely on sales from one particular product.

In hindsight, it seems as if it would have been a pretty simple decision to buy IBM back in the 1950s. But in reality, only one in a thousand small companies will ever become a blue chip. And the winners are almost never the $2 and $3 "hot tips" your broker calls you about.

The risks in picking the wrong small stocks are great. Big stocks' larger size is a great insurance policy against total disaster. For example, though it no longer dominates any growing markets in computing and is arguably many years into a long-term decline, IBM is still a solid enough outfit to be included in the Dow Jones Industrial Average. If you buy its stock today, you can rest easy that it will still be in business several years from now, even if you don't make any money with it.

In contrast, smaller companies are far more vulnerable to the effects of recessions, poor investments, competition and lousy management. For many of today's tiny tots, one bad quarter can sink the whole ship. Many promising small firms have also been derailed by the unexpected death of a key executive or board member. Large firms, in contrast, tend to be huge organizations run by many people, with the ability to replace key personnel when needed.

Small companies are often less well researched by Wall Street than larger ones. Unless you're careful, looming problems can go almost unnoticed until it's too late to get out. The equally dangerous flip side is that you might wind up buying a small growth firm at the very peak of its performance.

Low-priced stocks are infamous for being bidded up on the recommendation of a prominent Wall Street research house, brokerage, advisor, magazine, television program, computer service or investment newsletter. Then, once the excitement has died down, they plunge back to earth as the original investors bail out.

Often the biggest problem with buying individual small stocks is deciding when to sell. Almost everyone has made the mistake of holding on for too long, or selling before a small stock's full promise was reached. Others refusing to admit defeat ride stocks steadily down, down, down, rather than bail out and move on to something else.

There's no foolproof method for avoiding these pitfalls. Most investors have to make their mistakes on their own before they get a feel for how small stock markets work. Fortunately, you can dramatically increase your learning curve—and decrease the pain of experience—by following one simple rule: Stick with quality.

Don't buy on a promise. Spend the time needed to make sure there's something there behind your stocks before you go plunking down a single doilar. Research won't completely protect you against every possible contingency, such as the surprise loss of a key executive. But the knowledge you gain can save you from avoidable problems, thereby putting your best foot forward and maximizing your chances of ultimate success.

If you're not willing to do that much, you're better off buying small stocks through a mutual fund. If you are willing, you'll almost certainly have your share of major success stories in your portfolio someday. Also, as inflation comes roaring back in the latter 1990s, even your disappointments should reward you with big long-term profits.

The Quest for Quality

We've pinpointed five criteria for picking top-quality small stocks. Again, these criteria won't always ensure that you pick all the best small fry. Some stocks not meeting these requirements now will eventually do quite well, while others that measure up well will flounder in the years ahead. On average, however, stocks that stack up will do far better than those that don't. And when you invest in individual small stocks, you want to push the odds as much in your favor as possible.

You'll reap bigger profits and avoid more pitfalls by buying quality small stocks. Keep on top of each of these criteria by reading your stocks' annual reports, 10Qs or 10-K reports, or by looking them up in a resource like *Value Line* (found in most libraries) on a regular basis. Many companies now have their own "home pages" on the Internet, where investors can access financial and business information on a regular basis.

- *Rising earnings growth for at least ten years, or for as long as the stock has been publicly traded.* Rising earnings are what propel a small growth stock upward. Stocks with little or no earnings are an unknown quantity. They could turn out to be wildly profitable if their promise translates into rising profits. But there's nothing to cushion their fall if those expectations turn out to be empty. Generally, the best stocks are those with long-term profit growth rates of at least 10 percent.

• *Rock-solid balance sheet.* Bond ratings from Moody's or Standard & Poor's are probably the best ways to gauge a company's financial strength. Ratings of BBB (Baa2 for Moody's) or higher are preferable. However, because many small companies either have not issued bonds or are unrated, that may not be an option. For these companies, the best measure of a firm's financial health is how much debt it has, particularly relative to its "shareholders equity." Lower debt (20 percent or less of total capital) means the company will be able to cut costs during economic downturns. Higher-debt firms can be forced to dramatically curtail expansion plans should sales growth slow unexpectedly.

• *Free cash flow.* The company should have money left over after paying all of its expenses, including interest on loans and construction costs. This money is called "free cash flow." It can be used for stock repurchases, dividend boosts, to expand or buy out other companies or simply to beef up the company's investments. In all cases, shareholders benefit.

• *Rising operating margins that are at least within a percentage point or two of all-time highs.* This is gross profit from a company's operations, the best measure of how profitable a company is. A rising margin indicates that the company has secured a profitable niche market, in which its dominance will produce big profits in the years ahead. It's calculated by dividing a company's total revenue by total operating expenses (excluding debt repayments).

• *Relatively low P/E ratio.* A stock with high growth potential and a low P/E is a rare find indeed. Specifically, we want companies whose annual earnings growth for the past five years is no more than 50 percent lower than their P/Es. In other words, if a company has a five-year profit growth rate of 10 percent, and a P/E of 30, it's not acceptable. But if its earnings growth rate were 20 percent, it would be.

9

Money You Can Trust

Pounds, dollars, francs, yen, lira, marks, dinars, dilasi. Virtually every country today has its own currency. The soundness of each—how well it's accepted by the nation's citizens and by foreigners—depends to a large extent on the policies of the country's government.

The world's high regard for Germany, for example, has made the German mark one of the world's most secure currencies. In contrast, few would accept the New Zaire currency, which has an official exchange rate of 5,655 per U.S. dollar, even in that benighted central African country. The same thing goes for the Ukrainian karbovanet, which was recently convertible at a rate of about 168,000 per U.S. dollar.

Government policies are always subject to radical changes. That means any currency—even the German mark—could experience a sharp decline in value. The decline of the British pound in 1992, the Mexican peso in 1994 and the German mark in the 1920s are painful reminders that paper money meltdowns can and do occur.

There is one form of money that you can always trust: gold. Empires have risen and fallen, plagues have raged and inflation has soared. But the yellow metal has always held its "real" value. Those who kept a store of it have always been able to afford life's necessities of food, clothing and shelter—as well as its pleasures—regardless of the turmoil going on around them.

The lesson of gold's resilience is well known to most of the world. Burdened by tyrannical and confiscatory governments for centuries, Asians in particular are famous for using the metal as a store of wealth. Americans, on the other hand, are more used to thinking of gold as a speculative investment, soaring at certain times before plunging back to earth.

In the latter 1990s, the yellow metal will once again glitter for its speculative appeal. It will also prove to be a great store of value, protecting its owners against the ravages of hyperinflation. During the 1970s, for example, the metal rose from its controlled price of $35 per ounce early in the decade to $800 in 1980.

This time around, gold should rise toward an ultimate top in the $1,000 an ounce range. Best of all, you won't have to be rich as Croesus to take advantage!

Noble Gold

Why does gold hold its ground so well in almost any economic and political environment? Because it's the most noble of metals.

That's not a phrase from a "hard money" handbook or a survivalist mantra. It's a direct quote from the July 20, 1995, issue of the highly respected British science periodical *Nature*. The cover displays a sketch of golden molecules with the headline, WHY GOLD IS NOBLE.

The article is a bit technical, but you don't have to hold a Ph.D. in chemistry to get its main point: gold's utterly unique properties. Simply, no metal is more beautiful or more flexible or has more resistance to corrosion than gold. One small ounce of gold can be pounded out to completely cover the floor of a medium-size room (twenty feet by eighteen feet), without losing any of its lustre.

Gold's noble character has given it a unique ability to hold its value, no matter what the economic environment. Go back over any fairly long period of time. For example, in early 1934 gold was fixed at a price of $35 an ounce. By mid-1995, the metal was selling for about $380 an ounce. That elevenfold gain in price roughly matched the inflation rate over those sixty-plus years. Going back a bit further, let's paraphrase a couple of old proverbs: The relationship between gold and bread prices has been constant over the ages and an ounce of gold will buy a nice suit of clothes, just as it did in ancient Egypt and Sumer.

Gold's ability to hold its value has given gold jewelry a unique appeal for centuries. Asians—Chinese and Middle Easterners in particular—have revered it almost as long as there have been civilizations. They've used gold as a way to store, transport and hide wealth from brutal rulers. Today, approximately 45 percent of the world's gold is held by central banks as a reserve asset. Bankers know that, unlike any other currency, gold is money that will be accepted everywhere, anytime.

How has gold managed to maintain value throughout history? Because it's also peculiar in another respect. Despite all those marvelous properties, the metal has very few industrial or medical uses. And even for those there are cheaper substitutes. For example, gold is a great conductor of electricity, but other metals like copper do a much better job at a far lower cost. Medically, gold is occasionally used to treat nearly intractable arthritis. But this is not a big market.

The lack of industrial uses for gold means that no scientific development has or ever will replace it. Gold's value instead comes from unique properties that are valued for their own sake—beauty, flexibility and resilience. Those are irreplaceable.

No other commodity that's used for industrial purposes can say the same. In fact, most go the way of the vacuum tube. That's because when a commodity becomes too expensive, a new technology will develop a cheaper substitute. During the inflationary 1966–1981 period, the average industrial commodity—as measured by the U.S. Bureau of Labor Statistics (BLS) index of thirteen basic commodity prices—actually underperformed compared with common stocks and dramatically underperformed compared with gold and oil, in large part because high prices forced industry to develop substitutes.

Gold As Money

Gold's timeless value made it the mainstay of all major world economies from the early 1700s until the Great Depression of the 1930s. The U.S. dollar was pegged to the yellow metal until the early 1970s. Except for times of war, governments guaranteed the value of their currencies by pledging to exchange a set amount of gold for them. This system was known as the gold standard.

Under the gold standard, the amount of gold in a country's treasury had a major influence on its economic activity. In the United

States, every dollar printed had to be backed by a certain amount of gold. If foreigners and others wanted to exchange their greenbacks for gold, the central bank was required to deliver it.

This system severely restricted governments' ability to encourage or discourage economic growth. In fact, it sometimes forced them to act exactly the opposite way from what the domestic situation called for. For example, if foreigners had acted en masse to cash in their British pounds for gold, the British government would have been forced to raise interest rates to make the pound more attractive to investors and protect its remaining gold reserves.

This strategy would put the brakes on inflation and slow the outflow of gold. However, it sometimes had the unfortunate side effect of turning economic downturns into full-scale recessions. As Charles Kindleberger points out in his book *The World in Depression, 1929–1939,* during the early 1930s the threat of gold outflows forced central banks to keep credit tight even as their economies entered the Great Depression.

More than anything else, it was the massive unemployment and sluggish growth of the 1930s that ended the gold standard for most of the world's economies. Following World War II, economic ministers of the victorious democracies established the Bretton Woods currency system, named after the site of their conference in New Hampshire.

With Europe in ruins, the American economy was by far the world's most powerful. Consequently, under the Bretton Woods system all of the world's major currencies were pegged to the U.S. dollar, which itself was pegged to gold at a price of $35 an ounce. All the world's central banks were required to maintain a reserve of dollars and to exchange them for their currencies. The United States alone was required to exchange its dollars for gold.

The modified gold standard worked fine as long as America's economic dominance was absolute. But as the European and Japanese economies recovered and grew, it became harder and harder for the United States to carry the burden of global fiscal responsibility. Finally, in 1971, faster inflation, the widening trade deficit and a run on U.S. gold reserves forced then-President Nixon to abandon the convertibility of dollars to the yellow metal. The price of gold was decontrolled and American citizens were allowed to buy it for the first time since the 1930s. Since that time, gold has sold for whatever price the market will bear.

We doubt the gold standard will be restored anytime soon, even if inflation soars in the decade ahead. The main reason is that any attempt to move in that direction would require central banks to give up any control they now exercise over economic growth. Also, by requiring interest rate hikes to counter gold outflows, a gold standard would prevent the kind of inflationary policies that politicians will need to overcome the effect of declining living standards in the years ahead, in order to win reelection.

The gold standard does have its adherents, however, including dark horse 1996 ex–presidential candidate Steve Forbes. Should they succeed in restoring the gold standard, its restrictions would be combined with rising world demand for industrial commodities, declining real incomes and the lack of wealth-enhancing productivity gains.

That would add up to a serious deflationary threat. As we said, that's still highly unlikely, but it is a risk worth preparing for. That's one reason why you should not completely forsake bonds in the years ahead.

Whether or not the gold standard returns, the yellow metal will continue to keep pace with inflation. It's the only monetary asset that governments cannot create or destroy, no matter how inflationary their policies become. Consequently, the metal is guaranteed to retain its value in inflationary times. The higher inflation goes, the higher gold prices will go. That makes it a core investment for the next decade, when inflation will reign supreme.

Golden Signs

What kind of gains can we expect for gold this time around? It's impossible to make predictions to the dollar, but the metal should greatly exceed even its Wall Street proponents' expectations.

Between the mid-1970s and 1980, gold climbed from a low of $100 to a high of over $800 an ounce. The catalyst was the double-digit inflation that reigned for much of the period. While the value of U.S. dollars and most other currencies rapidly lost ground in real terms, gold held its own and gained speculative value as well.

As we pointed out in the first part of this book, the growing mandate for inflationary policies, a long-term bull market in basic industrial commodities and a huge monetary overhang make the potential for inflation in the latter 1990s much greater than even during the 1970s. That means gold prices could hit well in excess of $1,000 an ounce—more than two-and-a-half times current levels—by the turn of the century.

Any long-term buy-and-hold investment in gold, therefore, should be a big winner in coming years—just as buying stocks and bonds was during the great bull market of the 1980s and early 1990s. If you time your buys and sells well, you can do even better.

Check out our long-term chart of gold prices since 1980. Gold slightly outperforms inflation over the very long haul, including periods of low inflation. But during fairly short spurts of one to three years, its gains have been astronomical. The secret is to be on board during those times when gold is scoring multi-100-percent gains.

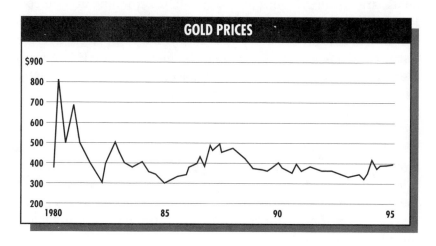

Gold's biggest upward bursts have come when the investing public's expectations of future inflation have been at their greatest. The peak of $800 an ounce in early 1980, for example, occurred after fifteen years of unrelenting inflation that most Americans felt would never end. Subsequent run-ups in the yellow metal in 1987 and 1990 were preceded by sharp upturns in the inflation rate that proved shortlived but scared most investors. In contrast, most of the rest of the time, gold has run in place, often lagging behind inflation.

The key to scoring big gains with gold in the latter 1990s and beyond, therefore, will be spotting the key signs that our inflationary forecast is coming to pass. Only rising inflationary expectations will trigger a big move in gold.

The best sign of rising inflationary expectations is the trend in "real," or inflation-adjusted, interest rates. Real interest rates are simply the difference between actual interest rates and the inflation rate. For example, suppose U.S. government bonds are yielding 7 percent and inflation has been running at a 3 percent annual rate. Real interest rates would be 4 percent (7 minus 3).

The higher real rates are, the more money lenders such as banks make. As a borrower, you have to earn more money to repay your debt. In contrast, lower real interest rates indicate that it's the borrower, not the lender, who has the upper hand.

Real interest rates essentially tell you what your real rate of return is for doing nothing. Suppose you have $10,000, government bonds are yielding 7 percent and inflation is running at 3 percent. Real rates are 4 percent, so all you have to do is buy government bonds with that $10,000 and a year later you'll be 4 percent ahead of inflation. You're effectively lending the money to the U.S. government, rather than investing it in a project or business. The same is true if you put the money in a bank—you're lending the money to a bank customer indirectly when the bank lends money to someone else.

When real interest rates are high, there's little incentive to do anything else but "loan" money in this way. As a result, high real rates are no friend of gold. Gold doesn't pay a return—it just sits there, forever beautiful but doing nothing. So when real rates are high, gold must not only keep up with inflation to be profitable, it must keep up with real rates as well.

When real rates are positive, as they are in our example above, gold has to gain considerably more than inflation. That historically has not happened. Because real rates are usually positive, gold doesn't do very well most of the time. Only when real rates are negative does the whole investment world turn upside down. That's when gold is suddenly a far better investment than lending money by buying bonds.

When real rates are negative, inflation is actually higher than interest rates. For example, if U.S. government bonds were yielding 7 percent and inflation were running at 8 percent, the real rate would be –1 percent. Prices in general are rising faster than interest rates.

Lending money when real rates are negative essentially means you'll wind up getting back less in real terms than you originally lent. For example, suppose inflation is running at 10 percent a year. You have $10,000 and a new car costs $10,000. But instead of buying the car, you put the money in the bank, which is paying 7 percent interest on deposits like yours.

At the end of the year you have made $700 and now have $10,700. That may sound pretty good. But unfortunately, 10 percent annual inflation means the new car now costs $11,000, and you are out of luck. High inflation made real interest rates −3 percent (7 percent yield minus 10 percent inflation). That made lending your hard-earned cash to the bank a loser's game.

When real interest rates are negative, the surest bet is gold. Our simple rule for buying gold is to buy when real rates are negative. During such times, gold goes crazy and you just can't own enough of it.

Take a look at our table. It shows clearly that historically the big gains in gold have always come when real rates were negative. In fact, since the yellow metal's price was decontrolled, it has multiplied its value five-and-a-half-fold during the total time in which real rates were negative. No other investment comes close.

Year	Average Gold	Real Rates*	Increase from Prior Year
		REAL RATES AND GOLD	
1972	$59	1.42%	—
1973	96	-7.70	62.7%
1974	160	-13.56	66.7
1975	161	4.73	0.6
1976	125	4.20	-22.4
1977	148	2.23	18.4
1978	194	-0.47	31.1
1979	308	-4.19	58.8
1980	613	0.08	99.0
1981	460	8.44	-25.0
1982	376	9.59	-18.3
1983	424	10.30	12.8
1984	361	10.16	-14.9
1985	318	9.79	-11.9
1986	368	12.19	15.7
1987	478	5.20	29.9
1988	438	5.33	-8.4
1989	383	4.83	-12.6
1990	385	3.27	0.5
1991	363	10.92	-5.7
1992	345	6.75	-5.0
1993	362	5.96	4.9
1994	385	5.77	6.3

*AAA bond yields minus ACPPI.

Focusing on the Negative

As the table shows, negative real interest rates are comparatively rare. In fact, real rates are positive almost all of the time. That's because lenders aren't crazy. They prefer to lend money when they can make a real return, not when a guaranteed loss is staring them in the face.

When real rates are positive, people only want to borrow when they can use the money to generate real returns above the real interest rates. A company will only borrow at a 4 percent real rate of interest if it knows it can earn a real return of at least that much on what it plans to invest in. Otherwise, management will put off its plans until it can self-finance its moves, until the potential profit increases or until real rates come down.

By curtailing borrowing, high real rates hold the growth of debt in check. That in turn helps the economy to run at a steady but slow rate. The only big borrowers are highly profitable companies and people forced to borrow out of desperation. Down-and-out individuals don't go to the pawn shop because they think they can earn more than 20 percent a month on the money they borrow. They go because they need cash fast.

As we pointed out in chapter five, debt in this country has continued to mushroom despite high real rates. That's partly because there have been things worth investing in like stocks. Unfortunately, it's also because an alarming number of consumers are borrowing just to keep up. Ultimately the only thing that can save them is a combination of negative real rates and high inflation. That will make their possessions, such as homes and even cars, more valuable, while simultaneously devaluing their debt.

In the mid-1990s, real interest rates have averaged a relatively high 4 percent. Given the world's increasing cry for growth, that won't last too much longer. Ultimately, the U.S. government will create negative real rates by printing ever more money, in a desperate effort to raise living standards the easy way.

At first, the additional money in the system will lower interest rates, making it easier to borrow more and pay interest on it. But only negative real interest rates will give today's debtors the "inflationary bailout" they need. Until then, consumers will fall ever-deeper into a hole.

Recessions are the result of not enough money being around. In the 1970s and 1980s, they were tolerable because the consumer's financial situation was not desperate. But as the wipeout of former President Bush in the 1992 elections showed, that's not the case today. Even with economic growth rising at a rapid 4.5 percent annual clip—adjusted for inflation—Mr. Bush got an historically low share of the vote. Voters are more dissatisfied with their economic lots than ever.

It's going to take vast amounts of money to make the majority feel solvent. As that's flushed into the system, interest rates will fall and inflation will rise. That means negative real interest rates and sharply higher inflationary expectations—and much higher gold prices.

The key to buying gold is to wait for negative real interest rates. The easiest way to tell is to subtract the most recent twelve-month rate of increase in the CPI—posted regularly in most financial newspapers—from the current interest rate paid on thirty-year U.S. Treasury bonds. If your answer is a negative number, bet the farm on gold!

Golden Investments

There are four major ways to buy gold. The most popular of these, collectible or "numismatic" coins, is discussed in chapter 14. The other three—gold bullion, mining stocks and commodity futures—each entail their own potential risks and rewards and are appropriate for certain investors.

The simplest and surest way to cash in is to buy gold bullion, either in gold bars or in bullion coins. The latter are minted 1-ounce coins, which typically sell for close to the value of their gold content, or "melt" value.

Provided you avoid leverage—borrowing to buy more—the worst thing that can happen to you buying bullion is that gold's price will languish. You're guaranteed to keep pace with the metal's moves.

If you buy bullion coins, a word to the wise is to watch the "premiums" charged by the various dealers. This is the price charged above melt value for the coins. Optimally, it should be no more than 1 or 2 percent. Prices of the most frequently traded bullion coins are listed daily in the *Wall Street Journal*.

Another thing to watch out for is bullion trading scams, which were prevalent during the last gold boom from 1986 to 1987. The bottom line is that if you're going to buy gold bullion or coins, keep it simple and stick with established dealers and brokerages. And be sure to comparison shop for the lowest fees and commissions!

When gold is flying high, gold is gold. During the past bull markets, no gold-related investment significantly outperformed gold itself. During the inflationary 1970s, for example, precious metals (gold and silver) rose at about a 33 percent annualized rate, while gold stocks trailed behind with a 28 percent annual gain. Covering the fifteen-year period 1966–1981, the comparison is 23 percent gains for bullion and 16 percent for stocks. So once real rates turn negative you probably can't do much better than buying bullion or bullion coins.

Unfortunately, as we pointed out earlier, gold bullion does not earn a return. It just sits there after you buy it. In contrast, gold mining stocks represent companies that can grow earnings even if gold prices stay flat.

Try this quiz. Suppose you can find nearly as much as you want of something that tends to hold its value. And thanks to technology, it costs you less and less each year to find this something. What do you have? The answer: a gold mine, literally.

Gold is found in small concentrations in all igneous (volcanic) rock. Quantities are small—only about five parts per billion. But there are a lot of potential deposits. As technology improves over time, the price of digging up these deposits is declining, as is the cost of finding new ones. Thus, established gold mines are really gold mines, or at least great long-term investments.

The mathematics of a well-run gold mine are pretty straightforward. Over the long haul, revenues rise because gold prices keep up with inflation and also because technology allows you to mine ever more gold. Costs over time don't rise nearly as fast as inflation, again because of technology and productivity gains. That's a recipe for very long-term profit growth.

When you throw in periods of positive real interest rates, gold stocks outperform gold bullion by a considerable margin. And here's the real surprise: not only do gold stocks do better than gold, they do better than most stocks. Our graph shows that since 1950, a time period that on balance has been very good to common stocks, gold stocks (when dividends are excluded) have actually outperformed typical industrial stocks.

Specifically, between 1950 and mid-1995, the S&P 400 industrial stock index has climbed approximately fortyfold, while the S&P gold stock average has climbed fiftyfold. Gold bullion during the period has climbed approximately elevenfold. Perhaps equally impressive is the fact that the typical gold stock has risen above its

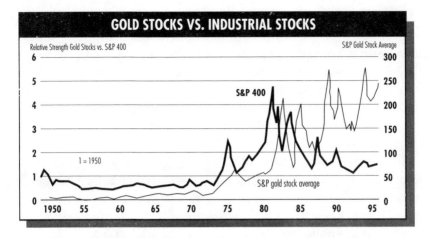

GOLD STOCKS VS. INDUSTRIAL STOCKS

Relative Strength Gold Stocks vs. S&P 400

S&P Gold Stock Average

S&P 400

1 = 1950

S&P gold stock average

1980 high even though gold in 1995 is more than 50 percent below its 1980 high. Even if you don't believe that inflation is coming back, gold stocks are a pretty darn good long-term investment.

Which gold stocks should you buy? Despite a near-depression for the mining industry in recent years, there are still scores of stocks to choose from, ranging from big producing senior shares to small exploring companies. As gold starts to boom in coming years, that number is certain to multiply.

For an indication of what the future gold stock market will look like, take a gander at the record of the gold bull market of 1986/87, when hundreds of new shares appeared almost overnight on the Vancouver Stock Exchange. Many of these mining companies multiplied their lucky investors' money many times almost overnight, as buy-crazy investors poured their funds into everything in sight.

The tragic thing was that, more often than not, investors were completely unaware of their companies' fundamentals. As a result, many bought what amounted to moose pasture. Once the boom ended in October 1987, these stocks plummeted back to earth. In fact, the carnage was far worse than that suffered on Wall Street.

This boom-bust cycle for small ("penny") mining stocks is likely to be repeated in the years ahead, quite possibly several times. The best idea for most investors is to avoid the group altogether, unless you're willing to spend the time necessary to really research the companies you're buying. In addition, you should never risk more than you can afford to lose.

In stark contrast are the biggest North American–based senior producers, shown in our table. These stocks also lost ground during the October stock market massacre in 1987, but all have held their own since. The reason: All are solid operations that are producing increasing amounts of gold, at ever-falling costs. Though the yellow metal has failed to rally significantly in recent years, they've kept making money. They're clearly the best long-term plays on gold around. All will be big winners in the inflationary years ahead.

One other group of gold stocks is worthy of mention: the South African major mining companies. These firms remain the world's most prolific produc-ers. Though they're no longer as dominant as they once were, these companies still account for more than a quarter of world production of the yellow metal and

GOLDEN MINES		
Company (Symbol)	Annual Production	Reserves
Barrick Gold (ABX)	2.4 mil oz	37.6 mil oz
Homestake Mining (HM)	1.6 mil oz	17.9 mil oz
Newmont Mining (NEM)	1.5 mil oz	23.2 mil oz
Santa Fe Pacific Gold (GLD)	0.9 mil oz	15.4 mil oz

*AAA bond yields minus ACPPI.

boast some of the richest mines on the planet. These companies also pay dividends, the exact amount of which varies depending on the gold prices that determine profits.

There's one major risk with buying South Africans that you won't have if you stick with North American mining shares: poli-tics. The country has emerged from its dark period of apartheid into a new age of democracy. Now under President Mandela, there's every hope for a prosperous future. Unfortunately, a huge percent-age of the country's population remains mired in poverty.

Unless the government can change that, unrest remains a strong possibility for the future. Should things go wrong, investors could lose money with South African mining stocks, even if gold soars. South Africans could make a better play than North Americans, should the country resolve its problems. But for our money, the North Americans are the more pure play on gold. Stick with them.

An alternative to individual gold stocks would be one of the great no-load mutual funds that specialize in precious metals. These may not give you the big gains of individual stocks, but they're cheaper to get into and they offer instant diversification by letting you own a piece of several dozen stocks at once. Two for all mar-kets are **Midas Fund** (800-400-6432) and **Vanguard Specialized Gold and Precious Metals** (800-662-7447), which has also proven itself in bad times as well as good. More aggressive is **United Services Gold Shares** (800-873-8637), a superstar in gold bull markets though historically a laggard when the bear comes to call.

The way to buy gold with the highest potential and greatest risk is with commodity futures and options contracts. A futures contract is a paper creation that allows you to make a heavily leveraged bet on price moves of a particular commodity, such as gold. For example, gold futures contracts are each worth 100 ounces of gold, or approximately $38,000 at a recent price of $380 an ounce. To buy a gold futures contract, however, you need only put up around $5,000.

To illustrate the power of that leverage, let's say you pay $5,000 for a gold futures contract with the price of gold at $380 an ounce. You now control a contract worth $38,000. Each contract is worth 100 ounces of gold, so every $1 rise in the yellow metal's price is worth $100 to you. If gold's price rises just $10, the value of your contract will rise to $39,000 from $38,000. But since you only put up $5,000 and made $1,000, you've made 20 percent on your money.

The flip side of leverage is that if gold's price falls by $10 an ounce, you'll lose 20 percent of your money. Consequently, this strategy is for risk takers only. Also, because gold's price can gyrate wildly in the short run, gold futures are not a suitable long-term strategy to cash in on the long-term gold bull market.

If you're interested in playing the futures game, the best idea is to contact one of the major futures exchanges like the Chicago Board of Trade (312-435-3500) or the COMEX (212-938-2000) and find out more about futures first. That way you'll avoid a lot of pain.

For everyone else, stick with big mining company stocks, gold funds and gold bullion. Your gains will still be staggering, and you'll be able to sleep at night too!

10

Toward $50 Oil

It's March 10, 2002. After a hotly contested special meeting, OPEC has boosted oil prices to only $50 a barrel. It was a hard-fought victory by the moderate nations over the hawks, who wanted to raise prices to $75 a barrel.

The G-11 group of industrial nations immediately protests the increase, the third in the past twelve months, and meets again to study use of conservation and alternative fuels. But double-digit inflation and $5 per gallon gas prices have made the leaders extremely unpopular at home, where the public is in little mood for sacrifice. In fact, a growing number of hardline nationalists are demanding military action against OPEC.

The leaders know that's impossible, given the reemergence of now oil-rich Russia's military power. Meanwhile, the Imam of the Islamic Arabian Republic—formerly Saudi Arabia—is calling for a renewed holy war against the Western infidel, and is threatening to close down the oil lanes in the Persian Gulf.

Sound far-fetched? It's easy to forget today with OPEC fragmented and energy prices at twenty-year lows, when adjusted for inflation. But the world was in a similarly dire situation less than twenty years ago, following the fall of the Shah of Iran. And today, thanks to a bottomless appetite for energy, especially oil, little new production and even less conservation, we're lurching perilously in that direction once again.

By the turn of the century, rapidly rising energy prices will become just as much a part of life as they were in the 1970s. That will fuel income-eroding inflation. But it will also provide a mighty profit stream to those who seize the opportunity in energy-related investments, especially oil and gas stocks.

Lessons of History

For the better part of a century, oil has been the world's most important source of energy. According to the International Energy Agency (IEA), fossil fuels currently provide around 90 percent of the world's primary energy demand (see pie chart). That share is certain to stay high as huge developing nations like China and India start trading in their bicycles for sleek Japanese- and American-built compact cars.

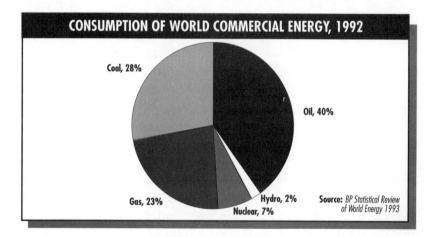

CONSUMPTION OF WORLD COMMERCIAL ENERGY, 1992

Coal, 28%
Oil, 40%
Gas, 23%
Hydro, 2%
Nuclear, 7%
Source: BP Statistical Review of World Energy 1993

Oil's dominance means that when its price rises, the cost of other fuels like natural gas soars along with it. As our graph shows, inflation-adjusted oil and energy prices have moved in twenty-year cycles since the beginning of this century. Once an upmove in prices is in place, it typically continues for about a decade. Upon reversing, prices then tend to slide for an equally long period of time.

Energy and oil prices play out these long cycles because exploring, producing and marketing oil requires a huge capital investment. Only when prices are high enough does it make sense to explore for and develop new sources of the stuff. Also, as the world

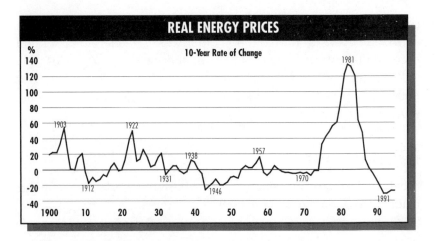

has ferreted out existing sources of oil, the time needed to locate new ones has increased.

When the supply-demand balance is tilted toward producers, it takes years before enough new supply comes on the market to shift the balance toward consumers—as lower prices. When the opposite is true, it may take years for supplies to decrease and demand to increase enough to send prices back up again.

Energy supply is concentrated in a few hands. Only a few companies or countries have the financial and technical resources to pay the cost of development. With few producers around, it's easy for suppliers to come together to control prices. That's why the supply of oil has always been controlled to some degree by cartels, whose power over the price waxes and wanes depending on supply and demand.

The last thirty years illustrate a typical oil price cycle. During the 1960s, energy was cheap all over the world. Low prices helped prolong the great economic boom that started in the late 1940s, but they also encouraged greater energy use. America remained one of the world's largest oil producers. But by 1970, demand had risen to the point at which we were heavily dependent on foreign producers, especially those in the newly emergent OPEC cartel.

Because of the huge expense needed to bring new production on line, OPEC's stranglehold on supply grew in the 1970s. Prices were steadily increased. Sometimes they spiked up, as during the Arab oil embargo of 1973 or when the Shah of Iran fell in 1978. By the end of the decade, oil prices were an incredible twenty times what they'd been at the end of the 1960s.

The decade of high prices, however, proved to be the undoing of

OPEC's power. Spurred by the incentive of huge potential profits, the world's major oil companies located massive new supplies of oil in the North Sea off the coast of Europe, parts of Asia, Latin America, Africa and off the Gulf Coast of the United States. By the early 1980s, those new fields were dramatically pumping up supplies.

At the same time, high energy prices made conservation chic in the developed world. In the space of a few short years, auto makers—particularly the Japanese—literally tripled the fuel efficiency of cars. Government subsidies and high prices induced thousands to better insulate their homes and install new high-tech thermal windows to cut down their heating and cooling bills.

The biggest blow to energy consumption in the early 1980s was the economy. Federal Reserve chairman Paul Volcker's war on inflation brought on the worst American recession since the 1930s. Energy demand dropped sharply.

By the mid-1980s, oil's upward price movement stalled and then decisively reversed. OPEC struggled for a few years to hold prices high by curtailing its output. But as their incomes fell, member nations began to "cheat" on their supply quotas, adding to the overabundance of supply.

Then in 1985, OPEC's power to set oil prices by controlling supply was shattered. Half a dozen non-OPEC nations were now major producers of the stuff. Demand had fallen off a cliff as slowing economic growth, conservation and a switch to alternative fuels like natural gas took their toll. Nuclear power began dramatically reducing oil's role in generating electricity.

The semblance of order that did remain in the oil market had been largely the result of Saudi Arabia's efforts. As owner of the world's largest oil reserves, the Saudis held a firm leash on radical OPEC nations like Iran, whose smaller reserves gave them the incentive to push OPEC for ever-higher prices. In the early 1980s, the Saudis kept oil prices high by cutting back their own production.

But in late 1985, burdened by a growing fiscal crisis and goaded by continued threats from more radical neighbors, the Saudis dropped their quota and unilaterally ratcheted up their oil production. Almost immediately, the price of black gold nosedived from the low twenties into the low teens.

Since that time, energy prices have remained low, except for a brief period surrounding the 1990/91 Persian Gulf War. That's sown the seeds for another mighty upsurge that will take place in the late 1990s.

The Typical Cycle

Some may argue that the last thirty years have been an aberration. However, energy price cycles have unfolded in remarkably similar ways since John D. Rockefeller's Standard Oil rose to power in the 1860s. Rockefeller gained a viselike grip on Americans' oil supplies—then used as kerosene for lamps—by controlling the pipelines out of the nation's then sole oil-producing region in Pennsylvania and building a global network.

Soaring demand (and prices) for black gold soon led to powerful new entrants—the Paris-based Rothschilds in Russia and Royal Dutch in the Far East—which broke Standard's monopoly hold. Meanwhile, coal-generated electricity emerged as a competitor to oil in lighting, further casting off the kerosene producers' hammerlock. Finally, the birth of Pure Oil in the United States launched a fully competitive alternative to Standard.

The advent of the automobile in the early twentieth century created a new use for oil, putting the power back into the hands of the producers again. This time the prime producing region shifted to Texas, where today's oil giant Texaco was born. Standard Oil was subsequently broken up by President Theodore Roosevelt's "trust busters" into modern day Amoco, Atlantic Richfield, British Petroleum U.S.A., Chevron, Conoco, Exxon and Mobil. But rising demand still gave producers the upper hand, through the infamous Texas Railway Commission.

The years that followed saw the increasing internationalization of oil production, as Americans, British, French and others all sought favorable "concessions" from third world nations to develop their oil resources. New supplies nudged oil prices down once more. That plus surging economic growth in the post–World War II world led to huge increases in energy demand. Meanwhile, the suburbanization of the industrial world led to rising demand for gasoline in autos. Utilities also burned increasing amounts of oil, due to environmental concerns about coal.

Eventually, the Europeans were thrown out of their former colonies. Britain was booted from Iran, which now wanted more control over its own industry. The result was a new opportunity for world energy market dominance by the "seven sisters," the biggest oil companies, which were mostly the greatly enlarged former parts of Standard Oil.

New supplies of oil again tilted the balance of power to the oil consumers in the 1960s. But as the economy grew, demand surged, setting the stage for the OPEC-led price increases of the 1970s. As before, those high prices encouraged competition and conservation, which once again shifted the advantage back to the consumer where it rests today.

Why an Oil Shock Is Coming

The energy crisis of the 1970s was born out of the energy waste of the 1950s and 1960s. Over the years, the industrial world's appetite for oil has dramatically outstripped its ability to produce it. American and European oil producers focused more and more attention on politically shaky regions of the world to make up the shortfall. Major discoveries in Africa, the Arab world and Latin America kept prices low, encouraging ever-greater demand and little conservation.

Dependence on these far-flung sources made the industrial nations increasingly vulnerable to uncontrollable political events. The result was the rise of OPEC, which brought the Western world to its knees with its campaign of rapid and violent energy price increases.

Unfortunately, today's situation has much in common with this picture. Americans still seem to believe cheap energy is a God-given birthright. Just let someone try to tell us not to drive gas-guzzling cars, or not to set our thermostats at 72 degrees in winter, or not to run our air conditioners throughout a cool summer night, or our high-powered stereos, on-line computers or thirty-six-inch-screen televisions. Just as during the 1960s, few pay any heed to where energy comes from.

Currently, the world is somewhere between phase 1 and phase 2 of the energy price cycle. Despite a strong run-up in oil prices in mid-1994, energy prices adjusted for inflation still sit close to twenty-year lows. Big oil companies' exploration for major new discoveries of oil and gas has all but ground to a halt. Instead, they're replacing reserves by purchasing existing fields on the cheap.

The world's fleet of oil rigs needed to drill for oil and gas offshore continues to age, and more and more wear out every year. But with oil prices still low, it makes no economic sense to either replace or repair them. Consequently, the world's capacity to draw up new reserves from the sea continues to contract.

Ditto for the world's refinery capacity, which is now running at some 90 percent of capacity even with Iraqi oil still constrained. With prices so low, it still doesn't make economic sense for the big oil powers to ratchet up their productive capabilities.

Other sources of energy grabbed a large slice of the pie in the 1980s, including nuclear power, renewable energy technologies and hydroelectric resources. But just as in prior cycles, nonfossil alternative fuels are also losing some of their luster to now-cheaper fossil fuels.

In California, for example, renewable fuels such as wind, solar, biomass (burning vegetable matter) and geothermal have long been favored, as utilities have been forced by government policy to emphasize them. California state regulators are now pushing plans to deregulate electricity that would put a priority on cutting electricity prices, to the detriment of conservation and these more expensive fuel resources. In addition, a nationwide movement is underway to repeal the 1978 Public Utility Regulatory Power Act (PURPA), which was created to foster small, renewable fuel plants.

Nuclear power is in a steep decline as the costs of meeting safety concerns, upgrading faulty plants and storing nuclear waste have been deemed not worth paying in an era of cheap energy. No new plants have been ordered for fifteen years and many are in the process of being shut down. Ditto for hydroelectric power plants, many of which now face a stiff challenge in their battle for relicensing due to the depletion of the salmon harvest and other environmental concerns. Even coal, still the mainstay of electric power production, has been made more expensive by the cost of complying with the Clean Air Act of 1990.

America's dependence on oil and gas for generating electricity is nowhere close to the levels of the 1960s and '70s. But it is growing once again. A switch back to other fuels plus the advent of electric and natural-gas-powered autos to control air pollution could further reduce oil demand by the turn of the century. But at best these steps will only slow the growth of our energy appetite, not reverse it.

Worse, even if we do manage to control our own appetite for energy and oil, it will not be nearly enough to control world demand. That's because, unlike in previous energy price cycles, we're no longer the world's only consumers.

Over the next fifty years, developing world nations like populous China and India—which are home to nearly one-third of the world's population—will suck down exponentially increasing amounts of energy. The London-based World Energy Council projects that the average person in China alone will expand energy consumption by 85 percent over the next quarter-century, while the average Indian's usage will grow 145 percent. This kind of growth in the world's two most populous countries seems inevitable as they build more industry, drive more cars and electrify more homes.

Demand in China should surge for years to come. Currently, China consumes just 5 percent of the energy per capita of the average American. As demand rises, domestic capacity's ability to meet it will shrink. China, for example, is the world's sixth largest oil producer. Nonetheless, the country became a net importer of the fuel for the first time ever in 1993.

Put that together with similar trends in dozens of other less developed countries, and you've got a literal explosion in demand for energy, especially oil. That trend will be compounded in coming years by the revival of the once-stagnant economies of Europe and Japan. The IEA now estimates a 35 to 45 percent jump in oil demand by the year 2010, a figure that's up sharply from the agency's earlier estimates. That kind of demand means sharply higher prices down the road.

There are two wildcard threats that could spark up energy prices even more. Number one is political instability in the world's largest producing countries. The former Soviet Union, for example, contains mammoth potential reserves. However, the now-separate republics' decrepit economies and often corrupt governments are preventing increasing amounts of it from getting to market. Even in Russia, existing oil production infrastructure is failing at the same time that money is drying up to exploit new discoveries.

In the ever-shaky Middle East, all seems quiet. In fact, Palestinians, Israelis and Jordanians are making peace. But beneath the surface the waters are quite murky indeed. Despite severe economic sanctions leveled against his regime, Saddam Hussein is rebuilding his once-humbled military power. Islamic fundamentalism continues to spread throughout the region, fueled by the inexorable trend of the rich getting richer and the poor getting poorer. Even Saudi Arabia is threatened.

Under one nightmare scenario, a new, more radical OPEC could emerge, dominated by militarily powerful Islamic fundamentalists with a reach extending into the Islamic regions of the old Soviet Union. Such an OPEC could for a time force prices as high as it wanted, throwing the world's energy importers into a bout of hyperinflation and ultimately depression. As in the 1970s, there would be little the United States and other Western nations could do, short of long-term measures like finding new reserves, switching to new sources of power and conserving energy.

Happily, we're still a long way from anything of this magnitude. The danger is that a major disruption of oil supplies is becoming ever more of a threat at the same time that the world is becoming ever more dependent on imported energy resources. That means increased risk of an oil price shock that would send the price of oil and other energy resources to unheard-of heights. That could make the Arab oil embargo of the mid-1970s look like a blip on the radar screen.

The second threat posed by foreign oil dependency could be even more serious for Americans. Ever since it burst on the world scene, oil has been universally priced in U.S. dollars. However, the dollar's value has now fallen consistently for nearly ten years against the Japanese yen and the German mark. That's increased the potential for a switch. Oil in the not too distant future could be priced in Japanese yen or German marks, rather than U.S. dollars.

Such a change would have staggering implications, particularly for U.S. inflation. According to the American Petroleum Institute, Americans' oil use for the first half of 1994 rose at its fastest rate in eight years, while our own oil production fell to its lowest level in thirty-six years! Providing the cheapest possible energy to improve business competitiveness is the order of the day, and conservation is once again scorned.

That energy "strategy" has forced America and other major industrial nations to import ever-larger quantities of oil from the OPEC nations. Imports as a percentage of our total oil consumption have now risen above 50 percent and continue to rise. And as the graph shows, America's oil endowment—all reserves past and future—continues to run out.

With oil currently priced in U.S. dollars, the erosion in the greenback's exchange value worldwide has had little effect on American inflation. That's because we can always pay for our appetite with dollars. If oil were priced in German marks, however, every downtick in the buck against the mark would ratchet up the price of energy. That would send an inflationary shock wave through our economy.

Neither of these wildcard events may happen. But at the very least, they dramatically increase the odds that energy prices are

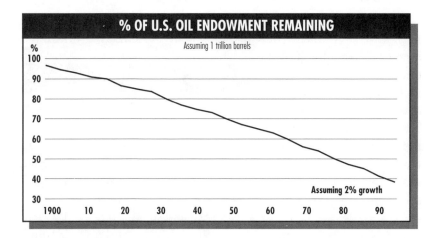

% OF U.S. OIL ENDOWMENT REMAINING

Assuming 1 trillion barrels

Assuming 2% growth

headed considerably higher. Almost completely unawares, the world is setting itself up for another energy price shock, or at least a steady, long-term rise in prices. The only real question is who will be the biggest winners.

Big Oil Buys

Oil is the world's single most important source of energy. Therefore, oil-related stocks are the best way to cash in on the long-term uptrend in energy prices. Natural gas stocks come in second, though most major oil firms are also major producers of natural gas.

The safest and surest bets are stocks of the major oil companies, the so-called seven sisters (see "Seven Sisters" table), which have dominated the world market for energy of all kinds during the entire twentieth century. These firms explore and drill for oil, refine it into myriad products and sell it as gasoline at the pump. This involvement in all phases of oil use means they profit from rising energy demand as well as from higher prices. Also, these firms' large size and strong finances make them flexible and safe in bad times, and they pay solid dividends to boot.

When it comes to getting energy out of the ground, American companies have far and away the world's best technology, management and financial and marketing power. Major oil companies will all reap their share of the spoils down the road.

The sisters also produce large quantities of natural gas. Gas is rapidly emerging as the world's fuel of choice. Technological advance has made it neatly interchangeable with oil for use in vehicles, as well as with both coal and oil in producing electricity. Burning it causes very little of the acid rain or smog that burning coal and oil do because it contains little nitrogen oxide or sulfur.

Unlike oil, gas is abundant in the United States, and thus enjoys the favor of the federal government. All told, gas demand growth could be twice that of oil over the next ten years. That's money in the bank for the seven sisters, which dominate its production as well.

SEVEN SISTERS		
Stock (Symbol)	Oil Reserves	Gas Reserves
Amoco (AN)	2.2 bil bbl	18.5 tril cu ft
Atlantic Richfield (ARC)	2.2 bil bbl	4.6 tril cu ft
Chevron (CHV)	4.2 bil bbl	10.0 tril cu ft
Exxon (XON)	6.6 bil bbl	42.2 tril cu ft
Mobil Corp (MOB)	3.4 bil bbl	17.7 tril cu ft
Royal Dutch Shell (RD)	8.9 bil bbl	48.7 tril cu ft
Texaco (TX)	2.7 bil bbl	6.2 tril cu ft

Five of the seven sisters were created by the 1912 breakup of John D. Rockefeller's Standard Oil empire: Exxon (formerly Standard Oil of New Jersey), Mobil (Standard Oil of New York), Chevron (Standard Oil of California), Amoco (Standard Oil of Indiana) and Atlantic Richfield or ARCO (Atlantic). The other two are Texaco, created during the early oil boom years in Texas, and Royal Dutch Shell, formed from the oil reach of the Dutch. Another major oil company is British Petroleum, which was born from the old Anglo-Persian Oil Company. The history of each of these companies is well documented in Daniel Yergen's Pulitzer Prize–winning epic, *The Prize*. Our table shows the oil and natural gas reserves of each of the seven sisters.

Going forward, all of these companies will enjoy rising profits from increases in the price of oil and gas, as well as from rising demand at the pump, which will bring more of their reserves into play. That translates into a steeply rising profit stream for years to come, and steadily growing dividends as well.

Their stocks can also gain one other way: As inflation heats up, energy is one of the few things that will keep pace and beat it. Because their earnings will rise along with energy prices, big oil stocks will become a prime inflation hedge in the eyes of mutual fund managers. Consequently, they'll sell at a premium to other stocks, just as they did during the 1970s.

One other group of oil and energy stocks is worthy of note: oil service companies. These firms provide the equipment, high technology and information needed for exploration and production of oil and natural gas, both offshore and on land. If we are half right on oil, this is where the really big money will be made over the next decade or so.

The two stocks in our "Oil Service All-Stars" table are the leaders in their industry. But they have weaker balance sheets than the major integrated companies discussed above. They also pay little or no dividends, and they tend to do much worse when energy prices are falling.

The experience of the past decade is all the evidence you need of this. Dozens of small oil producers have closed their doors. Even the major oil companies have dramatically slashed new production and exploration for reserves, preferring instead to acquire proven wells and properties. As a result, business has dried up for oil service firms. Survivors are now a downsized few.

That retrenchment has set the stage for a dramatic rebound by oil service firms. The industry's contraction is a major reason why it will be a long time before energy prices slow their upward momentum, once the bull market begins.

OIL SERVICE ALL-STARS	
Company (Symbol)	
Halliburton (HAL)	Oil field services, related engineering and construction with 40% of sales foreign.
Schlumberger (SLB)	Oil field services, related wireline, testing, cementing, marine seismic surveys, etc.

Much of the equipment used in the oil service industry is very expensive, for example oil rigs used in offshore drilling. With oil and gas prices so low for so long, it simply hasn't made sense to replace or upgrade existing equipment. As a result, the estimated existing fleet of offshore drilling rigs continues to shrink dramatically.

As oil and gas prices rise it will once again begin to make economic sense to upgrade and expand the rig fleet. That will probably take several years. In the meantime, the existing rigs will be in heavy demand from all oil producers. Ditto for other oil service equipment. For the oil service companies, that demand means they'll be able to push prices higher, giving their incomes an exponential boost.

In the 1970s, oil service firms' exploding earnings made their stocks red hot plays in what was otherwise a losers' market. Halliburton and Schlumberger are by far the world's dominant oil service companies. They were the biggest and best then. The same should be true over the next ten years as well. During the 1970s, oil service companies generated gains of over 30 percent a year for a total gain of over fourteenfold. While we obviously can't promise those kind of gains again, the potential here is enormous.

Those looking for a mutual fund should try **Vanguard Specialized Energy** (800-662-7447; $3,000 initial minimum investment), which holds a basket of energy producers and service providers. The fund is no-load, charges low fees, pays a moderate dividend and has a strong track record in both bull and bear markets for energy.

The End of the Cycle

Ultimately, the huge boost in energy prices we expect over the next decade will trigger an equally mind-bending decline. That's certainly been the case during every previous cycle. High prices always encourage greater development of new reserves and alternatives while encouraging ever-greater production. Gargantuan oil deposits are waiting to be exploited in Russia and China, and need only the lubricant of higher prices to grease the wheels of production.

Alternative fuels such as solar and wind will almost surely move to the forefront during an energy price upmove. And by law, at least 25,000 electric-powered vehicles will be on the roads of California by the year 1998, with ten times that many by 2003. Several other states now have similar electric vehicle laws in place.

All of these "solutions" to swing the supply-demand balance back to consumers will need time to have a real effect. In the meantime, they're coming up against the forces for higher prices that we've laid out in this chapter—forces so profound they've taken years to reach the point where they are now.

One further point: The need for politicians to stimulate worldwide growth at the expense of fighting inflation will also play into the hands of higher energy prices. As long as recessions remain taboo in politics, there will not be an economic slowdown to cool off energy demand and prices, as there was in the early 1980s. That could keep the current cycle going a lot longer than previous ones, sending energy-related stocks into the stratosphere.

11

Be Your Own Boss

AT&T, General Electric, IBM and other behemoths employ many thousands of workers worldwide. When they expand or contract, the communities where they do business can experience massive economic booms, or catastrophic busts.

Small companies, however, are the lifeblood of the economy. Almost twice as many Americans work for businesses with less than 100 workers than for companies with more than 1,000 workers. Our pie chart tells the story.

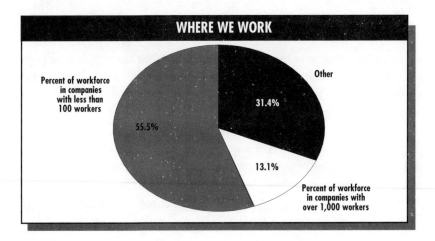

WHERE WE WORK

Other

31.4%

Percent of workforce in companies with less than 100 workers

55.5%

13.1%

Percent of workforce in companies with over 1,000 workers

Small companies' importance is even more pronounced when it comes to job creation. From 1975 through 1992, companies with less than 100 employees created some 19 million new jobs. In contrast, firms with payrolls of over 1,000 people hired only 3 million.

Small companies have been especially big providers of payroll growth during times of rapid inflation. For the period from 1975 through 1980, for example, the total number of workers employed at businesses with less than 100 workers rose by a whopping 30 percent. That was roughly twice the total growth of workers in companies employing over 1,000.

Unfortunately, the years since have been a bit tougher for the little guys. Just as low inflation has hurt the performance of small stocks for the last fifteen years, it's also damaged the health of small companies' business prospects. As our graph shows, since 1987 the small-business job pool has risen a paltry 7 percent, less than half the big-company job growth rate, which maintained its historic level of 15 percent.

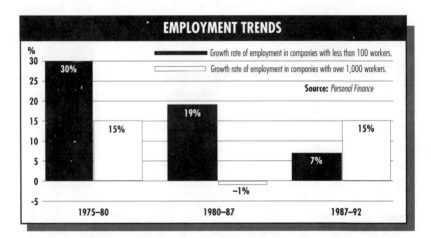

Small companies aren't hiring in the 1990s at anywhere near the rate they were back in the 1970s or even the '80s. Despite their huge layoffs, it's the big boys—not the small fry—who are doing the majority of the hiring now.

Our second graph shows another way small companies have declined in recent years. It tracks the growth in new incorporations—the actual creation of new small companies—since 1975. As you can see, this rate of growth has also been declining sharply in recent years.

The high and rising inflation we expect for the latter 1990s and beyond should mark a turnaround for small businesses, just as it

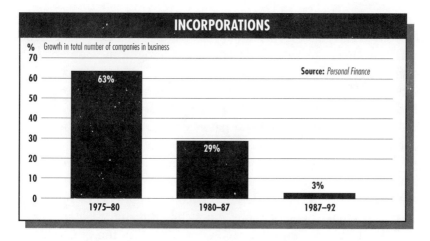

INCORPORATIONS

% Growth in total number of companies in business

Source: *Personal Finance*

63%	29%	3%
1975–80	1980–87	1987–92

will for small stocks on Wall Street. If you've ever wanted to start your own business, this is the time.

Inflation Is Your Friend

The period from 1975 to 1980 has been widely derided as the "Carter malaise" years of out-of-control inflation and high unemployment. Less well known is that those years were a true golden age for small companies.

During the latter 1970s, the number of companies in business grew a whopping 63 percent. In stark contrast, the so-called roaring Reagan era from 1980 to 1987—a time considered to be good for business—saw the rate of new company formations drop sharply, with only 29 percent more being formed. Since 1987, the total number of enterprises has increased by just 3 percent.

Small firms have been responsible for the majority of patents for new inventions for at least the last 100 years. To safeguard their products from competitors, companies apply to the U.S. government for patents, which give them exclusive rights to profit from the fruit of their labors for a set length of time.

The number of patents granted each year is an excellent way to measure the number of new inventions and processes that have been brought to market. By extension, it gives a good indication of the health of small companies and what kind of job growth we can expect for small business and the economy as a whole.

Written nearly three decades ago, and now unfortunately out of print, the best study of patents is still John Jewkes, David Sawers, and Richard Stillerman's *Sources of Invention.* The three authors examined sixty-one revolutionary inventions, including jet engines, insulin, power steering in automobiles, xerography (copying) and catalytic cracking of petroleum. Over 65 percent—or forty of the sixty-one—came from the hands and inspiration of either private inventors or small companies.

Small companies dominate patents because of innovation. Only one in a thousand small companies ever become big ones. The only way to succeed is to constantly change and adapt new products to new markets. In contrast, many large companies can take years to change direction and are often burdened with entrenched bureaucracies, which make new ideas and innovation difficult to put in place.

Take the microcomputer revolution, arguably the greatest innovation of the late twentieth century. As recently as the early 1980s, IBM reigned supreme in the computer industry with its control of the market for giant mainframe systems. Its research budget and market power dwarfed those of its few competitors. The "Big Blue" name was the industry standard and its earnings were growing at an enviable pace.

A little more than a decade later, IBM has hardly been a footnote in its industry's radical transformation from giant mainframe computers to compact personal computers. The winners of that battle were small companies that have since become large ones. Intel is now the undisputed kingpin of the microchip, while Apple's and Microsoft's innovative operating systems made it possible for novices to harness the power of the personal computer with ease.

Patent creation was robust in the latter 1970s, reflecting the

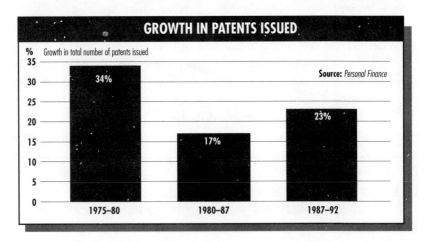

vibrant growth of small companies. Unfortunately, as our third graph shows, the number of new patents granted is still well off the torrid pace of the late 1970s.

There's no shortage of popular explanations for small companies' swoon of recent years. Pro-consumer regulations, litigation inflation and higher taxes have all taken their toll. Less of all three would doubtless be a great help to entrepreneurs today.

But the only thing that will really revive American small business is higher inflation. Small companies slump relative to large companies when the level of nominal economic growth is low and inflation is tame. The main reason is that slower growth means less demand and smaller markets for goods and services.

The Coming Boom

It's much more difficult for small companies to grab market share from a larger, more established one under sluggish economic conditions. That's because the bigger player has the power to underprice them on a broad scale to keep sales up.

With overall sales growth declining, the small company will be forced to slash prices, with a potentially devastating effect on its profits. Squeezed profits, in turn, force little enterprises to at least curtail new hiring. At worst, they have to slash payrolls to stay afloat.

In contrast, when growth is surging, small companies will have a much easier time selling their goods and services because the market for them will be that much greater. Large companies will not try to underprice but will instead be maximizing their own gains through price hikes. Small companies, in other words, thrive when pricing power is not at a premium in the marketplace.

The declining rates of growth in small-company employment, new incorporations and patents all confirm that small companies did far better during the inflationary 1970s than during the low-inflation 1980s and early 1990s.

Over the long pull small companies' growth has clearly been faster than that of large firms. Part of the reason is simple mathematics: a company with $1 million in sales has to add only $1 million more to double its revenue. In contrast, a $1 billion firm must find $1 billion in new revenue to achieve the same growth rate, a far more difficult task.

Consequently, small-company growth rates are higher in part because they're starting from a lower level. That advantage is secured when economic growth is on track and inflation is rising, since large companies will have a harder time squeezing small companies out of the market.

Also, faster economic growth and higher inflation typically go hand-in-hand with lower inflation-adjusted, or "real," interest rates. Low real rates make it easier for small companies to profitably borrow to finance their growth.

Low real rates, faster economic growth and higher inflation were in place during small companies' boom years of the 1970s. But ever since, the situation has been turned upside down.

Since 1987, small companies' growth rates have actually fallen below those of large companies. Over that same period, inflation slowed, real interest rates were high and annual economic growth has been slowed to a crawl.

A fortunate few like Microsoft have burgeoned thanks to being in the right place at the right time with the right innovation. They've continued to add workers and fuel the nation's economic vitality. Most entrepreneurs, however, have had to struggle to get by in a slow-growth environment where big companies dominate markets and earnings growth must be earned the hard way, by grabbing market share. That's why small companies' stock prices have badly lagged behind those of large companies over the past ten years or so.

The bottom line: The throttling back of economic growth to control inflation—the economic policy that has been in full force since Paul Volcker began clamping down at the Federal Reserve in 1980—has crimped the growth of America's small businesses. This in turn has slowed the technological advancement and job creation small companies provide, crippling the country's major source of economic vibrancy.

As inflation revives, small companies will perform better as they gain maneuverability. Rather than obsessing about cutting costs, businesses will be more interested in new ways to make money. Consumers will become less preoccupied with debt and job security and more focused on improving their quality of life. Everyone will become more interested customers of small, innovative companies.

Small companies are strong when the economy is growing faster and inflation is higher. The last time these economic fundamentals were in place was the last great inflationary era in this country: 1966 through 1981. This period included several bear markets for stocks and a crippling recession in 1973/74. Through it all, however, successful small businesses made millionaires out of many.

Over the next ten years, faster economic growth will open the doors of opportunity to a new breed of entrepreneurs. Opportunities will range from computer programming to manufacturing new consumer products. The owners of this new breed of businesses will reap profits beyond their wildest dreams.

Starting a Small Business

Going into business for yourself doesn't have to mean hocking everything you own, or even quitting your job. It just requires finding a market opportunity that matches your skills.

The possibilities are literally endless. Unfortunately, the risks of failure are also fairly steep. Less than one in five new small businesses lasts more than five years.

Two ways you can maximize your potential for success are information gathering and prior planning. The first step for a potential entrepreneur in planning is to ask yourself a few basic questions:

- What is your expertise? Make an inventory of your skills, education and experience. Decide what kind of services you can provide. Design a resumé for attracting clients.
- What market niches can you fill with your expertise? If you're a journalist, the easiest route for you will be writing. This could include freelance jobs, starting your own publication or writing a book. Computer programmers might consider consulting in their spare time. But be realistic. Remember, a director of personnel is unlikely to get much business as an auto mechanic and vice versa.
- Are you willing to commit the time? Even if you quit your "day job," starting up and running a small business can require huge amounts of time. It's not a 9-to-5 job! Leaky roofs, absent employees and clients who "need it now" are all part of the gig. Your leisure activities will have to come second.
- Are you willing to commit the money and do you have enough to get started until you start earning revenue? This is the num-

ber one reason why small businesses fail. Experts say you should be able to pay all initial expenses plus operating costs for a full year. Building a customer or client base takes time, but rent has to be paid from day one. Even a successful start-up can have a long wait before turning a profit.

Consulting is perhaps the most logical way for most people to start a business. You can capitalize on expertise you've built up in other jobs—particularly if you've been in a "knowledge worker" field requiring some level of advanced education, such as law, accountancy or engineering. Counsulting also requires almost no start-up costs for merchandise, office space or employees, at least until your operation has built up a bit.

The trend in American business toward downsizing and out-sourcing also favors the consultant business. Big companies frequently need help and are willing to pay for it from outside experts rather than incur the costs of hiring directly.

There's one other big advantage to consulting. If you've been in the same business for a while, chances are you've built a wealth of contacts. These will be natural clients as you get started.

Another option to consider for opening your own business is franchising. Accounting for a rapidly growing 34 percent of the nation's retail sales in 1990, franchises cover a wide range of businesses, with just as large a range of prices. They offer the advantage of a proven business idea, tested procedures and a nationally recognized brand name. You can also observe the business in operation before you buy.

There are numerous books available on the subject of franchises. One great source is the nonprofit International Franchise Association (IFA) (800-543-1038). It offers a free catalog of information available to potential franchisers.

Hundreds of books have been written specifically on the subject of starting your own business. Some of these might be helpful, provided the author has some knowledge of your field. Many simply repeat the obvious. In any case, you'll almost certainly be better off starting out with a few generic sources for how to set things up.

One of these is the Small Business Administration (SBA), which has over 600 small-business development centers. Their SCORE program provides free counseling from retired executives. They also operate the Small Business Institute, which in conjunction with over 500 universities provides management studies. Your local Better Business Bureau and Chamber of Commerce are two other places to contact.

No source can tell you everything. You'll have to put what you find out into the context of your particular situation. Remember, there's no substitute for legwork. After you've decided what sort of business you want to run, be sure to visit a similar business and talk to other entrepreneurs. Experience is the best teacher, so put theirs to work for you.

Tips on Taxes

There are two areas of opening a business where you'll want to step up your research a notch: tax preparation and building the right relationship with a bank. Either can derail your plans, so don't skimp!

Adequate tax preparation is essential to avoiding an audit that may possibly run you out of business. The Internal Revenue Service offers two tax guides for small businesses, both of which are required reading. Request "Your Business Tax Kit" and "The Tax Guide for Small Business" from your local IRS office. Following the guidelines therein should help you avoid most problems.

Here are a few of the red flags to avoid. Many would also invite a personal audit:

- A client reports that you receive different amounts of income than you report on your return.
- The amount of a deduction is out of line with the rest of your return.
- An item is reported on an "inappropriate" or unusual place on your return.
- If you've been audited before and there has been a significant adjustment, there's a good chance your business will be audited again.
- If your business is one the IRS has targeted for scrutiny. Recently, attorneys, taxicab drivers and gas station owners have been the target of a special IRS audit program.

Audits can take several forms. An office audit requires a visit to the IRS agent's office for review of certain documentation of your return. A correspondence audit requires only that you send in some documentation to answer a question about your return.

Both of these are relatively painless compared to a field audit, which involves an actual IRS visit to your office. These are eight times more likely to involve a tax increase than are other forms of audits. Most complicated are those involving the Taxpayer Compliance Measurement Program (TCMP), which are randomly selected returns the IRS uses to evaluate the extent to which taxpayers are complying with the law.

If you should get called in for an audit of your business, the rules of the game are the same as if your personal records were audited. Some hints for a smoother process are to arrive on time, be courteous and honest, don't make idle conversation, don't fill out financial statements without consulting a tax professional first, and request a second appointment if you still have questions. Also, remember that you can tape record any meeting with the IRS, and you can adjourn a meeting at any time to consult with a tax advisor.

Most businesses involve some start-up costs. That may mean taking out a loan from a bank. Before you approach one, assess what your first year costs will be as accurately as possible. Lenders generally need information on the following:

- Sales, expenses and profit projections for at least a year.
- Financial statements, including balance sheets and income statements, for several prior years (if available). If not, personal data will have to do.
- Background on key personnel.
- A detailed description of the business.

If you plan to personally guarantee the loan to your business (usually a bad idea according to most experts), you'll also have to provide information on your net worth and several years' tax returns.

When choosing a bank, remember that you're not just taking out a one-time loan. Most successful businesses will periodically need to borrow money for expansion and other needs. Choose a bank with which you can build a relationship that will build your business over the years.

Be sure to ask around for suggestions first from others in your business. The best choice will be a bank that's familiar with the ups and downs of your industry. Avoid banks that are unfamiliar with or ambivalent about your industry. Many businesses have been destroyed by lenders who decided it was time to stop servicing a particular business.

Evaluate banks by their level of customer service, financial stability (ask to see financial statements) and flexibility with your needs and by your compatibility with your prospective loan officer. The latter point may seem trivial, but personality conflicts have been known to destroy business relationships in the past. Don't let it happen to you. Also, compare interest rates, loan fees and other charges, and make sure you get the best rate you can.

Remember that everything is a trade-off. Large banks are more financially stable and can often offer lower rates than small ones. But smaller ones can offer more personal service and flexibility. Shop around.

There are also a variety of alternatives to bank financing for small start-up businesses. The Small Business Investment Company (SBIC) program, licensed and regulated by the SBA, makes capital investments in small businesses in the form of equity capital, guaranty-backed loans, long-term loans and buying preferred stock, and offers management assistance. Contact your local SBA for more information.

Starting up a small business is only part of the deal. As you develop a client base and begin filling work orders, you'll face many challenges along the way. Being a successful entrepreneur means relying on your brains, a lot of hard work and more than a little luck. And there are no guarantees you'll receive anything for your efforts.

But in the faster-growth, higher-inflation environment of the latter 1990s and early 2000s, small businesses as a group will thrive. If the boom period of the latter 1970s is any guide, thousands of millionaires will be made in hundreds of different small businesses.

Others won't reach quite that high, but will still make enough to stay well ahead of inflation, while their colleagues will struggle to stay afloat. If you've ever wanted to be your own boss, there's no time like the present to get started.

12

Real Values

"Go for the land; they ain't making any more of it," advised folk hero Will Rogers earlier this century. Almost everyone who heeded his words has profited. As the country's population has grown, real estate prices have maintained a long-term uptrend that will keep going for years to come.

Unfortunately for those who've held real estate over the last decade, no trend moves in a straight line. After soaring throughout the inflationary 1970s, property prices have taken a break during the low-inflation 1980s and early 1990s.

First to get hit was the Midwest. Slow growth, the closing of major industrial plants and falling commodity prices during the 1981/82 recession led to an exodus of jobs, money and people. Later in the decade, even the country's strongest areas had found their comeuppance. The 1980s' highest flyers—California, Hawaii and New England—are only now starting to emerge from major recessionary slumps. Property prices are nowhere near their old highs and in some places remain in a downtrend.

All that will change in the years of higher inflation and faster economic growth ahead. There are several major reasons why real estate will thrive in coming years. First, it's about as tangible or "hard" an asset as you can get. Its price rises as the value of money declines. Property values skyrocketed during the 1970s as inflation eroded the value of money. That's exactly what will happen in the latter 1990s and well into the next century.

Second, property is typically bought using a large amount of debt or leverage. Debt loses value when inflation rises, further enriching property owners.

Last but not least, faster growth and higher inflation make it easier for the average person to buy property. That makes it easier to sell real estate in all forms, which pushes up prices.

There are several ways to profit from the coming boom, ranging from risky partnerships to simply owning your own home. The surest and most lucrative play: selected real estate investment trusts (REITs).

The Real Thing

Thousands of middle-class homeowners saw their wealth multiply during the 1970s for one simple reason. Inflation and rapid economic growth triggered a dramatic increase in the value of their homes. Part of the good news about the coming inflation is that this will happen again over the next decade. Simply owning the home you live in is a surefire way to participate.

As inflation picks up steam, homeowners win two ways. First the value of their property rises, boosting their equity in it. That's because the value of money erodes, boosting the price of all real assets.

Second, the "real" cost of your mortgage loan will decline as money loses value to inflation. With interest rates still near historic lows and many real estate markets depressed, there may not be a better time to buy than now.

Overall, this is a fairly low-risk strategy. As the resident of a property, you're intimately familiar with its problems and key advantages. That will make it relatively easy to maintain and even upgrade, should the opportunity arise.

You can maximize your gains by using more leverage to purchase your property. In other words, by making as small a down payment as possible and borrowing the maximum amount you'll put yourself in line for the biggest gains in equity and you'll profit the most from the devaluing of debt.

This strategy is considerably riskier than making a larger down payment. Your monthly payments will be higher and, with little equity in the property, you could have a tough time selling in a pinch. If we're wrong about inflation, you could get burned by having a higher debt load. Also, you'll probably have to pay private mortgage insurance (PMI), adding to your monthly bill.

Those with the cash are probably better off using a leveraged strategy with investment property. That way, you can cut and run if a property investment turns sour, without the risk of losing your home.

There are several ways to pick out individual properties, all of which require doing a fair amount of research on your own. Most people start out the same way they'd look for a residence, by finding a location they like. Then the best idea is to seek out an agent who's familiar with the area to pinpoint the better properties around. The agent can also be invaluable in steering the deal through with a minimum of hassles.

As a buyer, you've certainly got nothing to lose by using a buyer's agent, since his or her commission will come out of the seller's pocket. In fact, in most cases, the buyer's agent will split fees with the seller's agent right down the middle. And if you plan on renting the space, agents can also help out with the details and the tenant interview process.

If you want to cut your tax bill and you meet certain qualifications, low-income housing investments are a great way to go. Rents are very low, but your cash flow will be subsidized by the federal government through tax benefits. You may be responsible for management.

Buying individual properties of real estate requires a large financial commitment. Before you make your move, you should consult with your accountant to consider the tax questions and your other obligations as landlord. Make sure you understand everything you sign at the bank as well. There are a number of books available from your local library on everything from property repairs to answering legal questions.

The REIT Way

Just like buying individual stocks, buying individual real estate parcels leaves you open to potential problems with that particular property. A rising tide of inflation will raise most real estate ships. But some problems could be so severe that they leave you out of the new bull market altogether.

The decline in a neighborhood's quality of life, the discovery of an environmental problem on your property, uninsured damage from some catastrophe, an unscrupulous renter and many other dangers can turn a real estate investment into a money pit in a big hurry, unless you're well prepared and constantly stay on top of your investments.

That's why many people prefer to hold their real estate indirectly as part of a package. Since the 1980s, brokerages have bundled together portfolios of residential, commercial and other properties and sold them as limited partnerships. Unfortunately, many of these are too highly leveraged with debt and are loaded with low-quality real estate. The danger of this situation was made all too clear when economic growth slowed down in the late 1980s and early 1990s—many partnerships folded and many investors lost their shirts.

You can still buy partnerships. But fortunately there's a better alternative for indirect real estate investing: real estate investment trusts (REITs). REITs are essentially professionally managed pools of real estate traded on major stock exchanges. Management buys, builds, manages, operates, rents and sells properties. REITs are ideal for income investors, since they're required to pay out almost all of their annual profits in dividends. And their diversification shields them from potential problems with a single property.

REITs are a relatively new innovation, created by the Real Estate Investment Trust Act of 1960. In fact, until the Tax Reform Act of 1986, REITs were required to use independent contractors to manage their assets, creating numerous procedural headaches.

Qualifying as a REIT now is considerably easier, with companies needing to meet the following legal requirements:

- Distribute at least 95 percent of otherwise taxable net income as dividends.
- Earn at least 75 percent of gross income from real estate in the form of rents, mortgage interest or capital gains from the selling of real estate.
- Have at least 100 shareholders, with no five shareholders owning more than 50 percent of the shares.
- Not engage in short-term speculative buying and selling of real estate.
- Be managed by a board of directors or trustees.

The result is a tightly managed pool of properties generating above-average income for shareholders. Managements have virtual carte blanche about how and where to invest. That's enabled well-run REITs to increase their dividends and earnings consistently, taking advantage of property's capital appreciation as well as boosting profit margins by efficiently managing properties.

There are three basic types of REITs. Some 87 percent are equity REITs, which manage and own a combination of residential, commercial, industrial and developing properties. About 7 percent are mortgage REITs, which as their name indicates own pools of property loans. The remainder are hybrid REITs, which own a combination of equity and mortgages.

High dividends have also made REITs somewhat interest rate–sensitive in the eyes of Wall Street, where some money managers trade them as virtual bond substitutes. Because their returns depend on mortgages and mortgage rates, mortgage REITs' profits are very sensitive to interest rate swings.

But equity REITs' long-term returns have historically corresponded much more closely to stocks than to bonds, both in terms of actual gains and in volatility. That's because they actually own individual properties. Just as with individual homeowners, faster growth and higher inflation appreciate the value of their properties, increase the rents they can charge and erode the value of the debt they borrowed to buy them. This ability to profit from growth will dramatically boost the worth of equity REITs in coming years, even as inflation devastates bond investors and mortgage REIT owners as well.

In the early and mid-1980s, for example, the dividend yield of New Plan Realty—the country's most established equity REIT—was about the same as it is today, even though bond yields were about twice what they are today. This means that when investors are bullish on New Plan and other REITs they require yields just half as high as those you get from a government bond. REITs could approximately double in value just to be priced the same in relation to bonds as they were in the 1980s.

As a group, the value of equity REITs rose consistently throughout the inflationary 1970s, generating total returns well in excess of inflation. There is plenty of room for the same to happen in the inflationary ten to fifteen years ahead.

Another attraction of equity REITs is the way they've dramatically outperformed other types of real estate since they first came to market. Look at our graph. The period from 1978 through 1993 covered a wide range of economic environments, including rapid inflation and a crushing recession. Equity REITs rang up an average annual total return of 16.4 percent over the period.

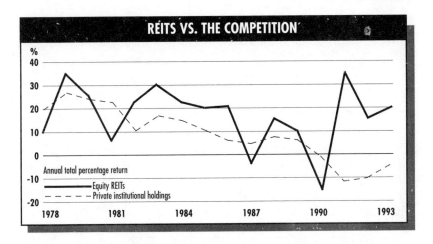

REITS VS. THE COMPETITION

In contrast, the value of real estate owned by institutions—as shown by the performance of the National Council of Real Estate Investment Fiduciaries index—rose by just 8.3 percent. And the value of other forms of real estate lagged as well.

In the future, REITs' returns will also benefit from what amounts to the "securitization" of the real estate market. Over the past ten years, REITs' total market value has risen from $7.7 billion to nearly $50 billion. The number of publicly traded companies has grown from only a few dozen during the 1960s to several hundred today, and that number is still rising. REITs' total market capitalization has doubled in the 1990s alone.

Despite their rapid growth, REITs' share of the total market value of investment real estate is still very small, only about 2.5 percent at end-year 1994, up from just 1 percent in 1990. Instead, most investment real estate in the mid-1990s is owned by large institutions such as pension funds and life insurance companies. These entities bought property in the past simply to round out their multi-billion dollar portfolios. Few have any experience managing it, so returns have tended to lag. In some cases, such as the insurance companies earlier this decade, results have been disastrous.

Bad experiences and the weak property markets of the early 1990s have convinced many large institutions to cancel or cut back on their ownership of properties. Their willingness to sell and unwillingness to invest more on favorable terms for property developers has provided a fertile field of top-quality properties for acquisition-hungry REITs. Many REIT CEOs are going one step further by convincing institutions to let them manage their properties for them. As REITs tap into this mammoth market, their property under management will multiply.

We project REITs' share of the total investment real estate market will expand into the 15 to 20 percent range over the next decade. Those new additions will mean soaring sales, higher profits and fatter dividends as efficiencies are implemented. Coupled with higher real estate prices, rising rents and the falling real cost of their debt, REITs should enjoy reliable annual double-digit profit and dividend growth well into the next century. In addition, top-notch REITs will keep dishing out some of the most generous income you can find.

The Right REITs

REITs do have pitfalls. Given the flood of new issues that have come to market over the past five years, many REITs' managements are less than experienced in different economic environments. In the rush to meet investor demand, some sponsors have packaged together inferior properties, many of which would have a tough time making it through a market downturn.

REITs' biggest risk is recession. Economic downturns typically depress real estate prices, since fewer people can afford to buy. More dangerous is the effect of slow growth on the rents REITs' dividends depend on.

Equity REITs with a large focus on retail properties such as shopping centers or malls are particularly vulnerable. They can be badly damaged if a retailer renter is forced to close up shop. The effect is magnified if the retailer is one of the mall's cornerstone renters (i.e., a major store that draws shoppers and smaller stores to the mall). The demise of many retailers in the mid-1990s and their effect on mall owners is a case in point.

A regional economic slump can damage REITs whose properties are overly concentrated in one particular geographic area. Highly leveraged (high-debt) REITs are perhaps most at risk, since their margin for error is less.

These risks mean that not every REIT will prove to be a gold mine in coming years. Selectivity is crucial. Here's a checklist for choosing the right REITs:

• *Top-flight management.* The most important criterion for choosing REITs is management that has proven itself over the long pull during both up and down markets. A consistent record of dividend increases over the past fifteen years, or at least no cuts, is one good indication of strong management. So is a steadily rising profit margin.

• *Concentration in economically stronger parts of the country.* The more jobs a state adds, the more its real estate should appreciate long-term. But as the experience of real estate near-depressions in New England and California during the early 1990s shows, bad times can strike even the healthiest places. There's just no substitute for some geographic diversification.

• *Diversification among several types of properties.* Owning a mix of residential, commercial and industrial properties allows a REIT to take advantage of the relative security of apartment rents and the faster growth of retail and other rents. Heavy weighting in one particular area—for example, retail—may not be dangerous provided management has a strong record of performance in all types of markets.

• *High occupancy rates.* One of the hallmarks of a healthy real estate portfolio is a high average rate of occupancy in its properties. A REIT can't make money unless it's getting rents. Allowing for normal turnover, an occupancy rate of at least 95 percent is optimal.

• *Low debt.* A low level of debt (20 percent or less of capital) gives a REIT much more flexibility to expand in bull markets, and take advantage of bargain buys of quality properties in bad ones. Low debt gives REITs maximum flexibility if times get tough to cut rents, make timely sales or do whatever else it takes to maintain their financial strength. Low debt also makes certain REITs recession beneficiaries. As interest rates fall, their prices will rise as investors chase their high, safe yields.

• *Low payout ratios based on funds from operations (FFO) with potential for growth.* FFO takes the unique aspects of owning property into account, making it the most important measure of REITs' profitability. The lower the FFO payout ratio (percentage of FFO paid out in annual dividends), the more a REIT can increase its payout over the long haul. FFO payout ratios under 70 percent are preferable.

THREE RIPE REITS			
	% Residential	% Shopping Centers	Primary Geographic Area*
BRE Properties (NYSE: BRE)	76	14	9 major Western cities
New Plan Realty (NYSE: NPR)	14	56	21 states nationwide
Washington REIT (ASE: WRE)	25	10	Washington, DC, area
*Percent of property owned.			

Our table lists three widely traded REITs, all of which are traded on major stock exchanges. They run the gamut in terms of type of properties owned and geographic focus. They're not the only REITs traded that meet all of the above selection criteria. But they are among the most solid companies in their industry. All are sure bets on REITs' long-term rise.

At the top of any REIT-buyer's list should be **New Plan Realty**, the flagship operation of the savvy Newman family. The Newmans have proven their mettle in both bull and bear markets, boosting dividends every year since the 1970s. New Plan's low debt load enabled it to snap up top-quality properties on the cheap during the recession of the early 1990s. In 1995, the REIT owned some 113 properties in nineteen states and it's adding dozens more each year. The largest REIT in America still has a very low debt load and is growing at a reliable double-digit rate.

Washington REIT has no debt at all. Management has compiled a solid record during recessions by sticking to quality properties. Washington's sole focus on the nation's capital and its Maryland and Virginia suburbs has lessened its appeal on Wall Street. But despite federal downsizing, its region remains one of the nation's strongest long-term.

Only 17 percent of capital-area workers are employed by the government in the mid-1990s, down from 60 percent in the 1960s. And the area's growth as an information and high-tech center will keep that number declining for years to come. Washington REIT itself derives just 5 percent of its revenue from federal sources. Management has boosted dividends every year since the 1970s. Steady, very reliable growth and no debt make Washington the safest of all REITs.

BRE Properties's bane in recent years has been operating in recession-plagued California, which has slowed growth and put dividends in doubt. Throughout the tough times, however, management was able to generate profits through efficiencies and quality control to keep the payout secure. Moreover, a jump in occupancy rates from 91 to 96 percent in 1995 is clear evidence that California and BRE are well on their way to recovery.

BRE's focus on multifamily apartments and expansion into neighboring, faster-growing states like Arizona, Oregon and Washington further ensure solid growth for years to come. Debt has been cut to the 25–30 percent range, ensuring adequate funds for further expansion and flexibility if the tough times return. The 1995 merger with California REIT is another major long-term plus.

Owning a basket of these first-rate REITs is a sure way to profit from the coming long-term bull market in real estate. All pay high, safe yields, will benefit from rapid economic growth and higher inflation and—based on their records over the past fifteen years or so—will be able to hold their own if the economy slumps again.

Unforeseen problems could arise, so diversify among at least two or three of these picks. And of course consider other REITs not listed here that meet our criteria. Many of these REITs also offer dividend reinvestment plans so you can compound your investment free of brokerage commissions. For more on REITs, consult *Value Line* (found in most libraries) or the National Association of Real Estate Investment Trusts (NAREIT) (800-3NA-REIT).

For those who don't want to buy individual stocks, there are also several REIT funds available. For example, **Fidelity Real Estate Investment** (800-544-8888; $2,500 initial minimum investment, $250 thereafter) owns a portfolio of REITs, supplemented with bonds and other real estate plays.

The fund has a solid record. But it does have a few drawbacks. It imposes sales loads and fees, and it bills you for expenses as well. This reduces your dividend yield. The fund does more trading than long-term investors would, and Fidelity funds also rotate their managers, a sometimes annoying practice that can threaten a fund's consistency. Also, returns have historically been better for those who buy and hold individual REITs.

Most investors are better off buying the five REITs discussed above. But no matter how you play it, an investment in real estate should prove to be quite rewarding in coming years, as inflation sweeps its way across the economy and markets.

13

Emerging Market Bonanza

More than half the world's people live in Asia. Yet since the dawning of the industrial revolution, the region's economies have lagged woefully behind Europe and America in terms of both living standards and raw size.

As we near the new millennium, Asia is casting aside its historic underperformance vis-à-vis the developed world. From Hong Kong to Singapore, many countries' economies are growing at two and three times the rate of the United States. Growing consumerism, still high savings rates, pro-business and pro-investment governments and rapidly expanding industrial capacity ensure that Asian outperformance will continue well into the next century.

The growing world mandate for faster economic growth will only intensify the trend. With more disposable cash, developed-world consumers will increase their purchases of electronics, machinery and other items produced in Asia. Higher developed-world inflation will force more companies to move operations to Asia, to take advantage of lower costs.

Very rapid regional economic growth will give the Asian stock markets the fuel they need to push ahead in the coming decade, even while the European and U.S. stock markets run in place. The easiest way to invest in them: the new Wall Street product World Equity Benchmark Securities, which we'll describe later.

Bucking the Cycle

Higher inflation means that big U.S. stocks will run in place for the next ten years. Making money means finding investments that will move countercyclically to them, such as oil, gold, real estate and small stocks. Stocks of emerging Asian economies also fit the bill.

One common misconception is that all stock markets move together. Our graphs are vivid proof that this is simply false. Markets may move together in the short run. But over the long haul Asian

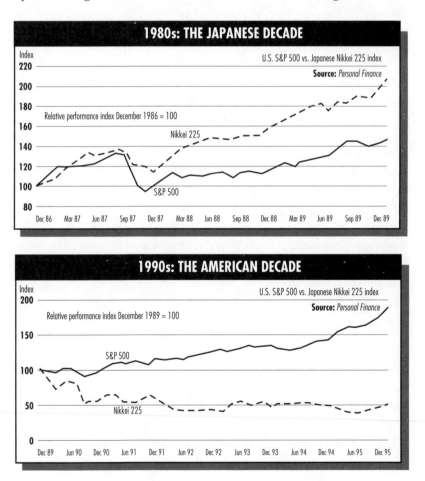

markets, even major ones like Japan's, march to a different drummer.

Between the mid-1980s and 1990, the U.S. market performed well. But the Japanese market was an unabated road to riches. It took the U.S. market a couple of years to recover from the crash of 1987. But that shocking debacle was just a slight blip on a major upward trajectory for the Japanese market.

The reverse has happened since 1990. Following a late-year sell-off inspired by Iraqi strongman Saddam Hussein's invasion of Kuwait, the U.S. market staged one of its greatest rallies in history. By contrast the Japanese market was a catastrophe, losing over 60 percent of its value from its highs. That pounding rivaled what happened in the U.S. market during the 1930s.

The conclusion: The U.S. and Japanese markets may have moved together somewhat. But over the last decade or so, they've more often moved separately than together. The next ten years or so won't be good for big U.S. stocks. But it will still be possible to make a fortune in Asian stocks.

There are three major reasons why Asian markets—including Japan's—will leave our own bourse in the dust over the next ten to fifteen years. First, the clearest advantage emerging economies and their stock markets have over the United States is that they are emerging. They represent economic bases that are much smaller than our own.

Smaller amounts of growth can therefore have a much more pronounced effect. A $100 billion economy needs only to add $100 billion in output to double in size. A $5 trillion economy needs to add $5 trillion, a much tougher feat.

Take a look at our table, which compares various economies in terms of per capita GNP. The massive Chinese economy would have to grow more than fifteenfold to be on a par with the United States, while the Indian economy would have to expand by about sixtyfold. Indeed, by the measure of GNP per capita there is no emerging economy that is even close to half as large as the United States'. Coupled with these countries' much larger populations, that gives them much more room to grow.

As capitalism has become more deeply rooted in these countries, their economies have rung up huge growth rates. As our table shows, during the 1990s every one of these economies has had growth rates that would make U.S. policymakers drool.

In recent years it has become accepted wisdom to say that the U.S. economy can't grow much faster than 2.5 percent without generating inflation. In contrast, emerging economies' small size means they can grow much faster without igniting serious inflation. Indeed, for most, a growth rate as low as 3 or even 3.5 percent would be called recessionary. In recent years the Taiwanese economy has managed growth well in excess of 5 percent without generating a lot of inflation.

The second reason why Asian markets will beat America's is the region's ongoing manufacturing boom. As we pointed out in chapter two, the U.S. manufacturing sector faces

EMERGING ECONOMIES		
	Per Capita GDP	Recent 12-Mo. GDP Growth
China	$1,738	10.9%
India	282	5.0
Indonesia	689	6.8
Malaysia	3,255	8.8
Philippines	791	5.7
Singapore	19,310	9.1
South Korea	7,368	6.8
Taiwan	10,460	8.5
Thailand	2,077	8.5
Germany	21,020	1.0
Japan	34,160	2.8
United States	24,580	1.3

Source: *Personal Finance*

stiff competition from emerging economies. American industry has responded by using productivity gains to cut costs, in order to stay competitive with lower-wage foreign countries. That in turn has depressed worker wages and living standards.

This is the downside to the triumph of capitalism—all major developing countries in the world are now competing with the United States. The result is much slower growth in the U.S. economy, the dominance of the service sector over manufacturing, falling living standards and widening wealth inequalities in society.

In contrast, Asia has enjoyed a manufacturing boom not unlike that of the United States following World War II. Workers in these emerging nations have enjoyed rising living standards as businesses there have boomed.

The region also has a far lower percentage of service workers and far more manufacturing workers, relative to its total workforce. Our second table shows the percentage of workers in the emerging nations' goods-producing industries—manufacturing, construction and mining—compared to that percentage in sample Western economies.

In chapter 2, we showed that one of the great problems of developed economies such as the United States is the inability to provide wealth-creating gains in service sector productivity. In fact, it's not even clear how to measure growth in the service sector. Given our country's huge reliance on service sector industries, that's given us a real problem generating wealth and raising living standards for all.

There are no such problems in economies where manufacturing goods is the dominant sector, such as emerging Asia. Productivity, productivity growth and overall growth are readily quantifiable, and they increase workers' living standards.

Developed countries' reliance on the service sector has made it very difficult for their economies to boost living standards through productivity gains. In the emerging countries,

FOCUS ON MANUFACTURING

	% of Labor Force in Goods-Producing Industries
China	78.7
India	72.4
Indonesia	64.6
Malaysia	51.4
Philippines	55.4
Singapore	32.2
South Korea	46.4
Taiwan	48.9
Thailand	72.2
Germany	38.3
Japan	38.1
United States	24.2

Source: *Personal Finance*

the heavy reliance on manufacturing means that productivity does help. Asian economies' growth is consequently going to be much more rapid and generate much more wealth than will growth in the developed nations.

Shop Till You Drop

The third reason why Asia will outperform the developed world is the region's nascent consumer boom. Since World War II, Asian companies have thrived by trading with the West, exporting billions of dollars worth of everything from plastics to electronics. That money has been the lifeblood of economies from Taiwan to Japan.

In 1995, however, something remarkable happened. These countries actually logged more trade volume between each other than with the developed world for the first time in recent economic history. The reason: Asia's burgeoning middle class is transforming the region's economies into major consumers of everything from cellular telephones and stereo equipment to denim jeans.

The self-sacrifice of the past that was historically so important to Asian nations' growth is giving way to a desire to enjoy the fruits of their labors. Fortunately for them, they can afford it.

Japan, for example, has become the world's banker over the past few decades by building up one of the biggest savings hoards in the world. The nation's historically low-cost, highly skilled labor force, strong work ethic and willingness to live for the future discouraged Western-style consumption of goods like stereo equipment in favor of savings.

Today, the Japanese have discovered they can well afford any and all such items, and in quantity. The same goes for the middle class in the region's other developing countries. As this vast pool of wage earners—that has piled away vast amounts of personal savings—begins to purchase the same goods and services that they have exported to the West for years, the pent-up demand will likely dwarf consumer demand in the developed world.

Once the trend is in place, history shows it can continue for a very long time. It's hard to believe today, but as recently as the mid-twentieth century, Americans and Europeans were big savers. Generations toiled so that their children could live better than they had.

Today, success has largely become synonymous with consumerism. The more possessions one can buy, the more successful one is considered to be in society. Spend, not save, is the order of the day. In fact, borrow and spend has become the national creed from the government on down to the smallest consumer. That's a major reason for our country's huge monetary/debt overhang, one of the three building blocks of the coming inflation. Stored wealth and savings rates within Europe and the United States have been falling over the past several decades, as consumerism has taken hold and expanded.

It's too soon to say if Asians will fall as hard for consumerism as Americans and Europeans have. But evidence is mounting that they are beginning to embrace the idea that they deserve to consume the goods and services they have produced for years. As this shift from save to spend continues, it will be a powerful force for economic growth in the region, just as it has been for decades in the United States and Europe.

Moreover, because their pool of savings is so large, Asians won't have to borrow and spend for some time. That will eliminate the upward check on their spending that debt limits create.

Companies that refocus their sales toward these new consumers in Asia will enjoy staggering growth over the next several years, as demand for goods that the developed world takes for granted accelerates further. That will be a further catalyst for expansion and growth of companies that once pursued only the developed-world consumer.

Small size, a reliance on manufacturing and the consumer boom mean that the markets of emerging Asia are on track to be huge winners in the coming generation, just as our market was following World War II. There are political risks, however. Should China turn to a xenophobic leadership in coming years, foreign players could lose heavily there, as well as in Hong Kong and probably Taiwan. Regions of countries like Indonesia and the Philippines are subject to political strife and occasionally open warfare. And Westerners are often shocked by the different ways of doing business in cultures far more ancient than our own.

Importantly, however, history clearly shows that once countries become even partly capitalist, they tend to stay that way. The only major exceptions in the last 200 years are Russia during the First World War—when the government was overthrown by the Bolsheviks due to its refusal to stop fighting in the face of a severe shortage of material goods—and Germany during the severe depression of the 1930s. As long as the Asian economies maintain their brisk growth, there's no chance of that happening there.

Ironically, developing Asia lacks one of the major risks now plaguing developed nations: severe inequalities in income. As our bar graph shows, emerging economies have a much more equal distribution of income than the developed economies.

As we said in chapter 2, the more service sector–oriented the economy, the more unevenly the rewards will be distributed among the workers. Asia's manufacturing-based economies, in contrast, are much more egalitarian.

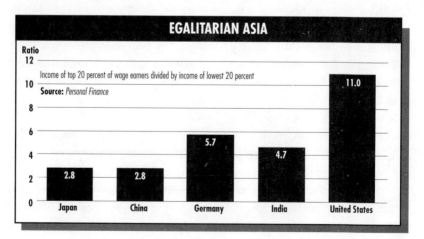

This more equal income distribution, in which the majority are participating in growth, is not just insurance against revolution. It also means there's less pressure on governments to inflate beyond the capacity of their economies to grow. And this means that growth—though very rapid—will not be so rapid as to be destabilizing. China, for example, has been able to clamp down on inflation in the past few years while still maintaining near double-digit economic growth.

Just as in the United States during the golden era of the 1950s and '60s, the biggest beneficiaries of Asia's boom will be stockholders. Closed in many places to foreign investors until recently, today virtually all of these emerging economies have a stock market in which investors from all countries can participate. These emerging stock markets will be the road to fabulous wealth in the 1990s and beyond. Over the next ten years, an investment in one of these countries will multiply your money, even while the inflation-battered U.S. markets struggle against the tide.

High Growth Cheap

Emerging Asian markets enjoy one further advantage over their developed-world counterparts: They're exceptionally cheap. Once you figure in accounting differences, most trade at much lower multiples to earnings and cash flow than do U.S. markets. That's because most have not participated in the bull market enjoyed by developed nations since the early 1990s.

Asia has long been both misunderstood and largely undervalued by the investment community. One reason is the U.S. dollar's decline since the late 1980s. As the buck has hit historic lows against the Japanese yen and other currencies in recent years, investors have sold off stocks of exporting companies within this region. The already depressed Japanese market saw further weakness that carried over to the other markets within the region, including those of Singapore, Malaysia and others.

The fear was that the buck's bashing would depress revenues for the region's exporting companies, since the equivalent amount of dollar sales would translate into fewer yen, Singapore dollars, Malaysian ringgits, etc. U.S.-based competitors would be able to undercut pricing, since their costs would be based in devalued dollars. Also, with slowed growth levels in the United States and

Europe, demand for consumer and wholesale imported goods would be less.

With the United States still a major trading partner with Asia—especially Japan—dollar fluctuations remain a risk. But with Asia now starting to trade within itself in a big way, the buck's moves will become far less important to the region's economic health over time. Until that happens, the Bank of Japan and other central banks are unlikely to permit the kind of colossal drop in the dollar that could really hurt major exporters.

Also, some countries such as Hong Kong actually peg their currencies to the U.S. dollar. Any dollar slide will make their products more competitive within Asia, as well as in the United States, when competing against unpegged countries like Japan. As for unpegged countries, U.S. investors should ultimately benefit from the dollar's decline, since the value of their holdings in those foreign currencies will increase.

The Best Countries

All of the nations of emerging Asia have some allure. Following Communist China's lead, countries like Vietnam are beginning to open themselves up to foreign investment and market reforms. Given their huge populations, generous resource bases, friendly governments and hard-working labor forces, even the most impoverished nations are strong bets to improve their living standards. Some will post growth rates that will dwarf those of the region's best economies now.

For the most part, however, it's best to stick with the better-known, better-developed economies. Capital markets are better established, traditions of market reforms more entrenched, savings are far higher and the road to success is much smoother. Four great examples are Japan, Hong Kong, Malaysia and Singapore.

Foremost on anyone's shopping list should be **Japan**. As we pointed out earlier in this chapter, the Japanese stock market has already proven its resilience in the face of U.S. market meltdowns by going its separate way over the past decade.

Japan's economy is considerably more developed than that of the rest of the region. Consumerism has already become a well-entrenched trend and the country boasts one of the world's highest per capita incomes. That's the result of a virtual rebuilding of the

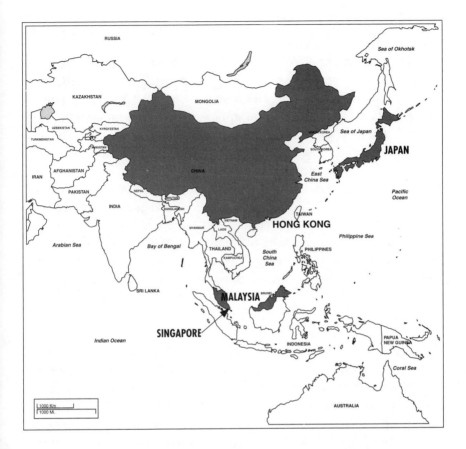

nation's economy and political system following World War II.

During the mid-1990s, Japan's banking sector faced a crisis reminiscent of the U.S. savings and loan meltdown of the 1980s, due to an unprecedented collapse in the bloated property sector. At the same time, the soaring Japanese yen depressed exporters' profits, particularly those who had made a living from exporting to America.

As a result, Japan today is a great economic comeback play in its own right. The country has virtually no inflation, a still very high savings rate and some of the most competitive companies in the world. As the yen stabilizes and the property market recovers, the Japanese market will show huge growth.

Japan's biggest attraction over the long haul is its proximity to and emerging dominance of nearby emerging Asian markets. Though they still face some resentment of Japan's historic aggressiveness in the region—particularly during World War II—Japanese companies are using the buying power of the yen to build massive new manufacturing facilities in other, much lower wage, faster-growing Asian countries.

Japanese stocks are also very cheap here in the mid-1990s. Differences in accounting make earnings comparisons difficult. But relative to their growth rates and cash flow, Japanese industrial companies trade at valuations that appear to be fractions of their U.S. and European counterparts.

Under British rule for all of this century, **Hong Kong** boasts one of the world's most modern infrastructures and powerful economies. It's also the best way to play the emerging growth of mainland China, home to one-quarter of the world's population and the globe's greatest potential consumer nation.

Reunification with mainland China in 1997 is a double-edged sword for the city-state. Being the doorway to China should make it easier for Hong Kong companies—which alone among the world's mighty multinationals are native Chinese speakers—to expand in the country. That should mean far faster growth for Hong Kong businesses.

The biggest risk is that reunification will bring heavy-handed regulation from Beijing in an attempt to rein in what some Chinese consider capitalism run amok. Some additional oversight is likely and the city's fledgling democracy's days are probably numbered. But China is unlikely to break its pledge to allow Hong Kong's corporations to operate as they are now for the next fifty years. These companies simply generate too much capital that's vital for the continued growth of China as a whole.

Reunification jitters will probably keep the market relatively cheap for the next few years, until the world gains more confidence in the island city-state's relationship with the Chinese government. That will make the Hong Kong market a great bargain, despite its historic correlation to the U.S. market in recent years.

Malaysia is a former British colony located on the southernmost peninsula in mainland Asia. Always a major trading area, this country has been the low-cost assembly and manufacturing center for Asia as well as a large producer of agricultural commodities.

When the country began to develop, its government imposed a restrictive marketplace, controlling foreign ownership of assets and levying huge tariffs on many foreign consumer goods. Combined with the country's rapid internal growth, the result has been a huge increase in savings and in the level of individual wealth in this nation.

Today, the government has begun to implement market deregulations, which given the population's new level of affluence should trigger a boom in demand for consumer goods. The biggest consumer in this country, though, is the government.

Malaysia is in the midst of a building boom that's arguably the biggest ever seen on planet Earth. Whole new cities are being planned and constructed out of what was once jungle. Airports and highways and other infrastructure projects are paving over old plantations. That's put a real strain on supplies of concrete and other building materials. Long term, there's cause for concern over too much construction and environmental degradation. But companies positioned in this sector will be well poised to profit during the coming years of what should be a long-lived boom.

Located south of Malaysia on the southernmost tip of the Malay Peninsula, **Singapore** is another city-state that was once a British colony. But unlike Hong Kong, there's no specter of the country losing its sovereignty. More of a company town than a country, Singapore has enjoyed economic growth in the high single digits for the past several years. Boasting an ultramodern infrastructure and a prosperous population, the city's key geographic location on vital sea lanes has made it a nerve center for world trade, a position it has held onto for centuries and is certain to keep for centuries more.

Singapore was named one of the world's most economically competitive nations in a 1996 survey by the International Institute for Management Development. Consumerism is more entrenched there than in the rest of the region, fueling internal demand. But like Japan, the country is also a major exporter to the rest of Asia, exploiting its competitiveness as well as its natural advantage of geography. In fact, its industry may be in the best position to meet the production demands of the Asian marketplace.

The government is viewed by many in the Western world as reactionary, particularly for its practice of caning lawbreakers. However, it has been very supportive of business development interests in its country and the rule of law is well respected, aiding both economic expansion and investors.

Despite these obvious strengths, the Singapore stock market has badly lagged that of its neighbors. For example, for a fifteen-month stretch ending in April 1996, the country's inflation-adjusted, or "real," economic growth rate topped 9 percent while its market index—the Straits Times Index—gained just 6.6 percent. In contrast, the U.S. market over that time gained more than 40 percent while economic growth was virtually nil.

How to Buy

Japan and Hong Kong both have established traditions of reliability for foreign investors. As a result, stocks of major corporations of both countries can be bought and sold on major U.S. exchanges as American Depositary Receipts (ADRs). These are essentially baskets of shares of foreign companies that banks package for U.S. investors.

ADRs trade like ordinary stocks on exchanges and the banks handle issues such as dividends and taxes. Some of the best of these are major Japanese companies like Hitachi and Sony, as well as Hong Kong Telecom. These shares will have their ups and downs, but long term it's hard to go wrong with any of them.

A better way to invest in these countries is with a product launched in early 1996 by the American Stock Exchange: World Equity Benchmark Shares, or WEBS. WEBS are basically indexes for a country. Like the Dow Industrial Average or Standard & Poor's 500 index in this country, they provide a benchmark or representative sampling of the stocks in each country. Selection is based upon the Morgan Stanley Capital International Indexes, which attempt to represent approximately 60 percent of the market capitalization of each country's market. As such, WEBS mirror the performance of each country's blue chips or largest companies.

Buying an index has several advantages over scooping up individual stocks in a country, or even buying a mutual fund. For one thing, WEBS are much easier to buy. They can be purchased or sold through any broker, like any ordinary shares of stock. As our table shows, each of the four countries profiled has its own WEBS share, the price of which can be found daily in American Stock Exchange listings.

Second, WEBS' large representation of markets gives investors a stake in stocks that would be otherwise impossible to buy. Rather than attempting to pick and choose

WINNING WEBS	
	Exchange: Symbol
Hong Kong WEBS	NYSE: EWH
Japan WEBS	NYSE: EWJ
Malaysia WEBS	NYSE: EWM
Singapore WEBS	NYSE: EWS
Source: *Personal Finance*	

individual foreign companies' stocks, with the often high commissions that can accompany such trades, professionals and institutional investors have for years been able to invest in index funds and tailored securities that match market indexes. WEBS give small investors the same advantage.

Third, mutual funds may seek a different course from the general market, which can sabotage your returns. But WEBS by nature are guaranteed to replicate what market indexes accomplish. As such, buying and holding them is a surefire way to capture the explosive growth of Asian markets.

Contact the American Stock Exchange for a prospectus and further information at 800-810-WEBS or on the World Wide Web at http://www.amex.com.

14

The Inflation-Beater Portfolio

To paraphrase an old Wall Street adage, successful investing means making the trend your friend. The trend for the next ten to fifteen years is faster economic growth and higher inflation. To profit rather than perish, you'll have to beef up holdings of real assets and lighten up on your financial assets like most stocks and bonds.

We've singled out commodities, small U.S stocks, emerging Asian stock markets, energy, precious metals and real estate as real asset plays that will make the grade in coming years. Below, we introduce a few more inflation beaters including some for income investors, who are otherwise very vulnerable to damage from higher inflation.

We've recommended these investments because they have one or more of the following three strengths: (1) Their values are tied to the price of a real asset in some way or another. (2) They've historically been big-time beneficiaries of faster economic growth. (3) They have the ability to outgrow inflation.

These strengths will enable our favored investments to beat inflation in all but the most extreme economic conditions. The proof is in our table headed "Best of the '70s," which compares the performance of our picks with that of inflation, bank savings accounts, long-term bonds and the overall stock market during the high-inflation decade of the 1970s.

The 1970s were characterized by relatively rapid economic growth interrupted by a sharp slowdown early in the decade. Inflation ran into the double digits first following the Arab oil embargo of 1974 and again after the overthrow of the Shah of Iran in 1978, basically due to soaring oil prices. Bonds finished the period under water by more than 4 percent a year vs. inflation, which was running at a blazing 8.1 percent. Excluding energy shares, the stock market lost more than 1 percent annually, as did cash.

BEST OF THE '70s		
	The 1970s Annualized Returns	
	Nominal	Real
Stocks (S&P 500)	8.40%	0.30%
Stocks (Except energy)	7.00	−1.10
Small Stocks	17.50	9.40
Long-term Bonds (Govt)	3.90	−4.20
Oil	26.40	18.30
Oil Stocks	14.20	6.10
Oil Service	31.00	22.90
Domestic Oil	19.20	11.10
Real Estate	10.10	2.00
Equity REITs	12.10	4.00
Commodities	11.00	2.90
Gold/Silver	33.10	25.00
Gold Stocks	28.00	19.90
Cash (T-Bills)	6.80	−1.30
CPI	8.10	

Source: Leeb Investment Advisors

In contrast, our favored investments beat inflation by a wide margin. Their gains also stacked up well against those of most blue-chip stocks during the bull market of the past fifteen years. Gold and silver's 33.1 percent average annual gain beat inflation by 25 percentage points a year. Oil service company stocks beat inflation by 22.9 percent. Small stocks rolled up an average annual return of 17.5 percent, beating inflation by 9.4 percent. Other plays also beat inflation by comfortable margins.

History never repeats itself exactly, but it is our best guide. The high inflation of the latter 1990s will resemble that of the 1970s and the same investments will certainly prosper.

There's no way to predict the exact returns any asset class will generate. One of the surest bets you can make is that the next ten years will not be exactly like any other. So the order of performance among our picks this time around will almost certainly be different. Equity REITs, for example, could theoretically be bigger winners than gold stocks. But if you load your portfolio with some picks from all of these groups you'll be certain to share in the spoils from each.

What to Do Now

How should you fit these inflation plays into your portfolio and how drastically should you act? The answer depends in part on your own preferences and financial goals. In other words, conservative players should stick with safer inflation plays while more aggressive investors should focus on the higher-reward/risk choices.

Also, long-term trends such as those we've described in this book take years to reach fruition. Economic growth began to accelerate in 1996, partly because of politicians' need to pump it up before the November elections. But the pressure on officials for faster growth worldwide will only intensify in coming years, evidenced by the continuing defeats of major political parties globally. At the same time, commodity prices appear to have awakened from their decade-long slumber, as faster growth has stimulated demand.

With these two building blocks of the coming inflation firmly in place, it's only a matter of time before they trigger the third building block: the monetary/debt overhang's money supply explosion. The timing could take several months or several years. But the result of faster economic growth and higher inflation will be the same.

The key is to begin taking incremental action on your portfolio now. That way, you'll avoid the need to make drastic changes that could cost you dearly in terms of brokerage commissions and tax liabilities, in addition to potential losses.

The first step is to start limiting your exposure to all those investments that generated real returns that were close to zero or below during the 1970s. One group is the stocks with the biggest market capitalizations—stock price times number of shares outstanding—or the "big caps." Big caps include household name blue chips like IBM. Note that big oil stocks are one big cap stock group worth holding onto.

Most bonds should also be avoided, though as we point out in the next chapter some still make sense as a hedge against deflation. You'll also want to keep your cash balances relatively low most of the time. Money market returns didn't keep up with inflation during the 1970s and they aren't likely to do so this time around either.

At the same time, you should begin adding the plays that did better during the 1970s. One of the most important conclusions that can be drawn from our table is how easy it was to generate great returns in the decade of the 1970s provided you were in the right investments. And small stocks (i.e., the smallest 20 percent of the NYSE) and gold stocks are no more difficult to buy than the IBMs of the world.

Mutual fund investors should begin shifting their stock holding from the traditional big company diversified funds to top quality choices specializing in small stocks. Those who are loaded up on, say, software companies for growth should turn their sights on oil service companies. Income investors should start swapping some of their long-term bonds in favor of inflation-beating income generators like equity REITs and big oil stocks.

Investors whose primary concern is growth will want to concentrate on plays with more explosive growth potential. In energy, for example, oil service companies offer the potential for much more explosive growth than the already gigantic "seven sisters." Those whose only goal is capital preservation can find a home in gold, the only money you can really trust over the long pull.

Inflation is still very low historically in the mid-1990s, and until we see a major recession the stock market will avoid a major bear market. Moreover, following the last great economic and market turning point—gold's meltdown in early 1980, which anticipated the fifteen-year drop in inflation—it took a long time for the new reality to catch up to stocks and bonds.

In 1984, when the economy was several years into a profound disinflationary trend, long-term bond yields were still well above 10 percent. Investors were still pricing bonds as if inflation were headed back to 7 or 8 percent when in fact inflation had been declining for several years and was headed for 2 to 3 percent.

This time around stocks have continued to surge for more than two years following the bond market meltdown of 1993/94. Gold remains stagnant, though bonds have repeatedly failed to break out to new highs.

Consequently, it will be some time before the three building blocks of inflation reach full force. But investors should make sure their portfolios are adjusting in the right direction. Specifically, most or all of your holdings should ultimately be able to beat inflation, whether they're income or growth plays. And don't wait too long to act.

As we've said, the trends of rising commodity prices, the mandate for faster economic growth and America's huge monetary and debt overhang are already well established. Slowly, perhaps imperceptibly to most, inflation is starting to reassert itself. Once that becomes obvious to all, inflation-beating investments will no longer be bargains. Here are a few more inflation plays that are ripe for the picking.

Collectibles Collage

Searched through that old junk drawer lately? Treasure hunted in your attic? If not, you may be overlooking a fortune.

One person's garbage is another's collectible. Someone else might be willing to pay good money for those old baseball cards, stamps, coins, paintings or anything else you might not want. In fact, you name it, chances are someone collects it.

The next ten years should be boom times for many collectibles. The reason: Just like gold or real estate, they're tangible assets. They gain value just as paper money loses it. That's what happened during the 1970s, and it's what lies in store for the latter 1990s and beyond.

There are literally hundreds of kinds of collectibles. Numismatic or collector coins are one of the most popular. Many of these have the added advantage of being minted from silver or gold, which makes them a play on the metals themselves as well.

As coin dealers are fond of pointing out, many people have literally made fortunes from buying and locking away selected numismatic coins. During the 1970s and again during the gold boom of 1986/87, certain coins multiplied their value twentyfold and more, as investors clamored to own them. Unfortunately, once the mania collapsed, so did the prices of many of these coins. In fact, some of the hottest numismatics of the 1986/87 buying binge are today scarcely worth more than the metal used to make them.

The above example is actually a typical cycle for all sorts of collectibles, and it points out the biggest danger of investing in them.

Never buy collectibles just because you think you're going to make money. Before you plunk down dollar one, develop an interest in what you're buying. In other words, make sure you wouldn't mind owning it for a long time if no one else thinks it's worth as much as you do.

All of the great collectors of history have loved their collections first. Making money was purely secondary, if considered at all. In fact, many made what were considered to be remarkably bad investments at the time. Would-be collectors should enjoy owning what they're buying.

You might decide to collect rare embroidery, cars, paintings, sculpture, books, farm implements, antique furniture, china, silverware, plastic cups with a certain logo printed on them, or something far more obscure. For the more popular collectibles like numismatic coins there are clubs, Internet computer forums, magazines, books, specialty stores and any number of other sources of information to help get you started—and keep you going. For less popular items, you'll have to dig a little bit deeper.

Start out by making small purchases. You'll make mistakes, and a less expensive one is easier to rectify. Also, if you decide you don't want to collect a certain item, it'll be easier to unload your collection. Learn how to recognize and buy quality items. Make sure what you're buying is in good shape. Damaged goods, such as a dog-eared baseball card, are worth far less than those in mint condition.

The single biggest way to lose money with collectibles is getting caught up in a speculative mania. While gold and real estate automatically gain value during inflationary times, a big part of collectible prices is what others are willing to pay. The key factor here is scarcity, or the perception of it. In other words, if it's tougher to buy genuine Indian Shivas, their price will go up because of it.

The basic illiquidity of collectibles—the difficulty of buying and selling them—gives them an additional speculative quality that's not shared by other real assets. In good times, the lack of sellers can send their prices soaring far further than those of ordinary gold coins, for example. On the other hand, when prices start to dip and everyone wants to sell, illiquidity means there will be few buyers. Prices crash far more dramatically than they do for real estate.

A great example of a collectibles mania boom and bust is the fabled seventeenth-century Dutch tulip bulb fiasco. Crazy as it sounds now, much of the world was caught up in a buying frenzy for tulip bulbs, which were originally imported by the Dutch from the Near East and then planted in Holland. The inevitable collapse of prices wiped out many a would-be collectibles speculator.

Looking ahead to the next ten to fifteen years, it's certain there'll be many such "tulipmania"-type booms and busts in the collectibles business. Each time, something will seem like a sure thing and its price will seem to rise forever. The fever will be further fueled by higher inflation. And just as every stock market buying mania collapses, so will every collectibles buying binge go bust.

In sum, many collectibles will do quite well in the inflationary latter 1990s, gaining value as money loses its value. But only investors who carefully buy what they know and like will benefit. Everyone else is better off sticking with gold, real estate, energy and other less esoteric real assets.

Inflationary Income Investing

Fixed income investors usually finish last during inflationary times. As the value of money drops, interest rates rise. That makes the interest payments, dividends and other cash streams paid by bonds and income stocks worth progressively less.

During the inflationary period from 1965 through 1981, bonds threw off an average total return—including interest payments—of 6.1 percent. That was a full percentage point behind average annual inflation for the period. Bond yields rose from the 4 percent area well into the double digits. Other traditional income investments, such as utility stocks, fared just as poorly, due to their huge borrowing needs.

The inflationary latter 1990s and beyond are also shaping up to be rough going for many income investments. Simply put, faster inflation will push up interest rates. This will erode the value of any fixed cash flow stream and trigger heavy capital losses to boot.

Fortunately, there is a way for income investors to win in the years ahead: Make sure what you buy has the potential to keep up with and even surpass future inflation. Specifically, that means income investments must either be tied to the value of some real asset or have the ability to grow their dividends or interest payments at least at the rate of inflation.

Possibilities include the real estate investment trusts discussed in chapter 12. These dish out essentially all of their income to shareholders in dividends. Faster inflation will boost the value of their properties as well as the rents on them. That in turn will boost REITs' principal and payout streams.

Another good choice is selected high-yield or "junk" bonds. When the economy sputters, weak companies typically have a rough go meeting their obligations. Investor confidence wanes and junk bond prices plunge. But faster growth enhances the credit-worthiness of weaker companies, improving investor confidence that the high interest payments on their debt can be paid in full.

In times of faster inflation and growth, investors can count on high yields and, ironically, considerably more safety to principal than ordinary bonds provide. No-load mutual funds like **Vanguard High-Yield Corporate Bond Fund** (800-662-7447) are the best way to invest—they let you buy a diversified portfolio with comparatively little money down.

Other possibilities include bonds whose values are tied to the price of a real asset. Good examples are convertible bonds of gold mining companies. As explained in the last chapter, gold stocks are big winners when the yellow metal is on a tear. Mining company convertible bonds pay regular semiannual interest and are also exchangeable for a set number of shares of stock at the holder's discretion. Consequently, their values rise when gold prices do. Examples include Amax Gold $3.75 Senior B Convertible Preferred (NYSE: AUPrB), Battle Mountain Gold's $3.25 Convertible Preferred (NYSE: BMGPr) and Echo Bay Mines $1.75 Convertible Preferred A (ASE: EBIPrA).

The best of the big and safe blue-chip stocks for income investors are the big oils discussed in chapter 10. Basically, healthy growth induces consumers to use more energy, particularly for driving. This tightens supplies relative to demand, pushing up prices. Because they produce, refine and distribute oil, the biggest oil companies thrive when the economy is running faster. Oil prices also rise along with inflation, boosting big oils' production revenues.

During the 1970s, big oil companies were one of the very few groups of major stocks that kept investors well ahead of inflation. For the decade, big oils scored average annual total returns (dividends plus capital gains) of nearly 15 percent. That was about twice as high as the total returns of the nonenergy stocks in the S&P 500 index.

A final group of investments to consider is selected energy utility stocks. Historically, utilities as a group have been big losers to inflation for two reasons. First, Wall Street buys them for income. When inflation and interest rates rise, the value of their dividend streams falls and investors sell. Second, the electricity and natural gas industries are very capital intensive, requiring big outlays to build new facilities and hook up new customers. Rising inflation hurts utilities by making it more expensive to borrow.

Ongoing industry deregulation, however, is changing the relationship between utilities and inflation. The advent of competition will allow some companies to grow faster at the expense of others. Also, more competition means that prices of these essential services will come to be set by market forces, rather than regulators. In other words, as energy prices rise across the board, so will deregulated electricity and natural gas prices charged by utilities, and utility profits.

The most promising utilities are those that are best set for competition and that also explore for and produce natural resources. They'll continue to pay an inflation-beating stream of dividends. They'll also gain from price increases in the coal, natural gas and oil they produce. Our table lists four great prospects.

HIGH ENERGY AND INCOME			
Stock (Symbol)	Type of Utility	Resource Operations	% of Income
Black Hills Corp (BKH)	electricity	coal, oil and gas	46
Energen (EGN)	natural gas	natural gas	30
MDU Resources (MDU)	electricity, natural gas	coal, oil and gas	61
Questar Corp (STR)	natural gas	oil and gas	41

These good utilities also have another advantage that's not shared by any of the other real assets or inflation-beating income investments discussed in this book: they operate secure essential service businesses. That gives them the ability to profit should our forecast for faster growth and higher inflation take longer to materialize than we expect.

That's only a dim possibility for the coming years, given the massive problems the American economy faces. In fact, it's debatable whether we could really stand a deflation without a full-scale economic collapse, given the large amount of debt we've piled up. But as we will explain, deflation is something you'll want to be insured against. That means having some utilities as well as traditional bonds, the subject of the next chapter.

15

Why You Should
Still Own Bonds

Here's an alternative future: The year is 2002 and President Newt Gingrich has just declared victory in the long-running budget wars, projecting America's first federal budget surplus in nearly forty years.

Following Uncle Sam's frugal example, the rest of the economy has cut its debt load as well. Unfortunately, for most people this hasn't been a matter of choice.

Balancing the budget has helped to bring down interest rates, just as its proponents always said it would do. In fact, it's helped squash the inflation out of the economy. For the first time in more than seventy years, the United States is running a deflation, in which prices are falling and money is actually gaining value year after year.

That's great news for those with ample savings—and no debt. Every year they're able to buy more with the money they have, instead of losing ground to inflation. But for everyone else, times are tougher than anyone can remember. In fact, even the wealthy aren't too happy: The stock market has crashed and burned and shows no signs of bouncing back. Values of real assets like real estate and gold have collapsed. Bonds have had a field day, but only for investors who have managed to avoid the surging tide of corporate and municipal bankruptcies.

Ironically, the reason for the pain is rooted in the cause of the deflation: When the stock market crashed in 2001, the federal government decided that controlling inflation and balancing the federal budget were more important than "bailing out the Wall Street fat cats." So, the politicians refused to pump more money back into the economy, as they had done after the short-lived crashes of 1987, 1990 and 1997. Instead, they stuck to a tight monetary and fiscal policy.

This sucked billions of dollars out of the economy precisely when it was needed most to keep growth going. Though considered wasteful spending by some, this cash once went to build roads, feed families, provide health care and finance military research projects. The vacuum it left had a ripple effect throughout the rest of the economy. People lost jobs and income, curtailing their spending habits. Anyone doing business with them, the banks that lent them money, the communities where they lived and their families also suffered a drop in spending power.

Deflation also sent "real," or inflation-adjusted, interest rates to sky-high levels. That made it very difficult for individuals and corporations to borrow money to finance expansion. It also made it very difficult for most people to repay the debt they already had, and defaults and bankruptcies are becoming increasingly common.

Imbued with the ideology of deficit cutting for years, many of the leaders are only waking up to the facts. But the result is, in effect, a full-blown economic depression—the worst since the 1930s. Unemployment has skyrocketed into the mid-teens, businesses are failing in record numbers and even bread lines are reappearing.

Coming as it has on the heels of an almost thirty-year decline in real incomes for Americans, the new depression has made the public angrier than ever. All across America, people are hanging President Newt in effigy and comparing him to another man who presided over a crippling depression in the previous century, Herbert Hoover.

Pundits say the ruling Republicans will be lucky to keep even 100 seats in the upcoming congressional elections. But the unpopular, divided Democrats aren't likely to benefit either. Instead, extremist alternative parties have been gaining ground in earnest, including one with a "send the immigrants home" message that beat both major parties in California's recent statewide elections.

Sound shocking? Fortunately, this alternative scenario is still highly unlikely. As we've pointed out in earlier chapters, faster inflation is still by far our most likely future, due to the combined trends of rising demand for commodities worldwide, a worldwide mandate for faster economic growth and the huge monetary and debt overhang in our economy.

But just as it's a thin line between love and hate, the difference between galloping inflation and catastrophic deflation or depression is slender. In fact, the very same forces that will produce rapid inflation in the next decade could, under slightly different circumstances, actually create the opposite condition—deflation and depression.

It's certainly happened that way before. The crippling recession of 1973/74, for example, occurred smack dab in the middle of the high-inflation 1970s. The result for the stock market was one of its worst meltdowns in history, with the average share shedding about half its value.

In the 1920s and the 1960s, the economy reached levels of debt similar to today's. In the 1960s, Federal Reserve chairman Arthur Burns pumped up the money supply in earnest. The result was the runaway inflation of the 1970s. However, the economy was able to pay off its debt and keep growing. In the 1920s, we weren't so lucky. Government failed to inflate and the economy sank into that generational catastrophe known today as the Great Depression.

There's only one investment that really gets a charge from deflation, and even depression: bonds, specifically those of the highest credit quality. America may avoid a calamitous depression in the years ahead. But if one does occur, bonds are the best and only real insurance against it.

Buying a bond is essentially lending money. As we pointed out in chapter 9, lenders make more money when real interest rates are high, which is most true during times of deflation. Lenders and bondholders lose money hand over fist when real interest rates are negative and inflation is rising.

Bonds were big winners during the low-inflation 1980s and early 1990s, actually beating stocks for much of the period. They were a disaster in the high-inflation 1970s, and they're on track to be losers again as inflation heats up in the latter 1990s. The low yield of 5.75

percent on the bellwether thirty-year U.S. Treasury bond, reached in late 1993, is a mark that's likely to stand for a long time.

But should the economy enter a period of severe deflation and even depression, bond yields could sink as low as 3 or even 2 percent. That would mean a near tripling of bond prices before the trend played out.

In this chapter, we explore the possibility of a deflationary depression, and what could cause one. We show why bonds hold their ground during such catastrophes and point out the best ways to buy them.

Causes of Deflation

Deflation is the opposite of inflation. Money is relatively scarce, so prices of almost all goods and services fall. Real asset values also plummet. Real interest rates skyrocket and debt becomes very difficult to repay. If unchecked by central bank increases in money supply growth—which lower real interest rates and make debt easier to pay off—this trend will lead to loan defaults on a massive scale and bank failures, which in turn shrink economic growth further.

Under the gold standard, deflations occurred regularly as countries were forced to adjust their domestic economic policies in line with international gold flows. The catastrophic experience of the 1930s Great Depression ended reliance on the gold standard by most of the world, allowing central banks to prevent future depressions through more flexible policies.

Since then, Japan has been the only country to experience a deflation. The massive decline in asset values, particularly real estate prices, has taken its toll with several bank failures. The country's central bank has been able to prevent a full-scale depression by inflating its money supply at a rapid clip.

Japan's ability to dodge the depression bullet is in large part due to the strong Japanese yen, which has allowed officials to act aggressively without fear of setting off a crisis of confidence in the country, as Mexico did with its December 1994 devaluation. Unfortunately, other nations with weaker currencies might not have that luxury should they enter a deflation.

America's last major deflation took place in the early 1930s. The catalyst was the market crash of 1929, which wiped out billions of dollars in equity literally overnight. At that point, the Federal

Reserve was restricted from pumping up the money supply by the shackles of the gold standard.

At the same time, the federal government was straitjacketed by President Herbert Hoover's insistence on maintaining a balanced budget, despite the economy's screams for stimulus. Hoover's treatment of the "bonus army" that came to Washington is a testament to his fanatical devotion to a balanced federal budget.

As the economy sank deeper into the Great Depression, destitute people from all over the country came to Washington, D.C., to collect a rumored bonus that would be paid by the government to veterans of World War I. Rebuffed upon arrival, the so-called bonus army proceeded to build a tent city close to government buildings. Their goal became to force the government to pay them the desperately needed bonus.

The human misery around him, however, did not convince Hoover that he should break his balanced federal budget. After months of simply trying to wait them out, he sent young General Douglas MacArthur to break up the bonus army's camp. MacArthur's militaristic zeal in carrying out his task resulted in one of the most violent actions ever taken by the U.S. government against its citizens.

With neither the Hoover administration nor the Fed willing to stimulate the economy, the money sucked out of the system by the stock market crash was never replaced. The deflation continued to rage out of control—and the economy sank deeper into a depression.

What are the chances of a repeat performance? As before, the trigger would certainly be some kind of major deflationary event—such as another stock market crash—and a mistaken response by the government, which would compound the problem by tightening credit, as it did in 1929.

Why would a stock market crash be deflationary? The answer lies in the history of the crash of 1929. There's been as much speculation about the causes of the crash as there was investment speculation before it occurred. But most market historians agree on one thing: The 1929 crash and its deflationary aftermath would have been much less severe if fewer Americans had hocked the house to buy stocks.

Back in those days, margin requirements were a mere 10 percent. In other words, you could buy $100 worth of stock by putting up just $10. This magnified gains and losses far more than today's 50 percent minimum margin requirement.

A 10 percent move in a stock bought with a 50 percent margin, for example, would produce a gain of 20 percent on your money. That same 10 percent gain in a stock bought with a 10 percent margin would double your money. Unfortunately, leverage is a double-edged sword. If you bought a stock with a 10 percent margin and it fell 10 percent, your equity position would be completely wiped out. In a full-blown market sell-off, heavily margined investors are forced to dump positions on fairly small downmoves in stocks. This creates more selling, and even bigger drops in stocks.

In the months leading up to the October 1929 crash, everyone from taxi drivers to insurance salesmen was buying stocks, lured by the upbeat national mood and the low margin requirements, which let them own a lot of stock for a small amount of cash. The risks of using such leverage were largely ignored, since stock prices had been rising for several years and almost no one expected the good times to end. As a result, the public was excessively leveraged by the time the crash occurred, resulting in a mind-numbing meltdown with severe repercussions throughout the economy.

At first glance, the direct leverage in the market of the mid-1990s is not nearly as excessive as it was during the 1920s. Thanks to higher margin requirements, the late, great bull market has not been fueled by wide-eyed speculators buying stock by putting down ten cents on the dollar. Instead, the prime mover has been Joe and Jeri Sixpack sinking ever more of their savings into what they increasingly view as a sure thing—stock mutual funds with good records.

Unfortunately, today's stock market is quite hugely leveraged indirectly, and that's every bit as threatening. The typical investor of the mid-1990s is not borrowing specifically to buy stocks. But he and she are still borrowing at the fastest pace in history. Thus far in the 1990s, consumer debt has been rising at a far faster clip than consumer income. Some years, it has risen even faster than the appreciation in financial assets.

What does consumer debt have to do with the stock and bond markets? A lot. Though they're not margining their stock investments per se, Americans are increasingly borrowing money while they're investing their cash in stocks. In effect, their debt is backed by their equity investments. And in a very real sense, the big move up in the stock market is being supported by huge increases in debt.

Should the stock market collapse as in 1929, that debt mountain could come crashing down, setting off a major deflationary depression.

What Could Cause a Depression

Only one thing makes the situation today less dangerous than during the 1920s on the eve of the Great Depression: experience. During the '20s, the government did not realize the deflationary implications of a stock market crash when debt was so high. Now we've hopefully learned the lesson that greater debt loads mean a greater chance of deflation following major market sell-offs.

The lesson was certainly not lost on Federal Reserve chairman Arthur Burns during the 1960s. He inflated the debt-bloated American economy of the 1960s, thereby setting off the inflation of the 1970s. Burns decision is today widely derided by monetary historians. But it must be pointed out that he did avoid that worst of economic calamities—a depression.

The lesson was also heeded by current Federal Reserve chairman Alan Greenspan. Following the October 1987 crash, he and his cohorts abandoned the war on inflation they had been waging for most of the year and cranked up money supply growth once again. Much later it was revealed that this swift, decisive action very likely prevented a wave of bank failures that could have created an economic depression. As it was, economic growth continued at a strong pace and the market eventually recovered.

Greenspan's efforts were aided by the fact that the stock market in 1987 was still largely a game played by "Wall Streeters." When the market fell, Wall Street trembled and shook but stocks were still only a small portion of household assets, much less than real estate, for example. Also, despite the crash, stocks still ended the full year of 1987 up by a fraction. Lastly, bonds went up in value, and bonds then were a very important part of the household balance sheet. Stocks' wipeout, therefore, did not eliminate that much money from the economy.

Unfortunately, the situation is far more dangerous today. Stock ownership, according to many surveys, is much more broad-based than ever before, including the 1987 and 1929 peaks. As we pointed out above, consumer debt as a percentage of income is also higher than ever before. Over the past three decades, installment debt has climbed to over 16 percent of income from about 13 percent.

Worse, many of today's investors are totally unfamiliar with bear markets. Most are completely wedded to the buy-and-hold philosophy that worked so well in the low-inflation 1980s, but that will be such a total disaster in the decade ahead. Even the relatively few who did live though the crash of 1987 have not experienced a year of double-digit declines, such as plagued the inflation-wracked 1970s. When all was said and done, 1987 was not really a bad year. Rather, it was like taking a turn too fast in a car but coming out OK because no one was in the other lane.

In contrast, rapid inflation will create jagged stock market volatility in coming years, making years of 10 percent–plus declines equally certain. At those times, stock-dependent, debt-heavy, inexperienced households will be especially vulnerable to going bust. The resulting deflation could be so explosive that even the best-intentioned government might have trouble containing it.

The biggest risk of deflation and depression in coming years is that government won't even try. Instead, politicians could be goaded by interpretations of voter polls into pursuing contractionary fiscal policies, precisely when they should be following a very stimulatory economic policy.

Our forecast for faster inflation in the next ten to fifteen years is to a large extent based on the premise that governments will continue to act rationally in the years to come. In other words, they'll increasingly try to enact policies to fire up economic growth in order to raise living standards and get reelected. This will produce more inflation. Pro-growth action is likely to be especially strong whenever the economy starts to slow a bit. Again, that's because of the lessons we have learned from the 1930s: severe recessions coupled with high debt are a recipe for calamity.

Unfortunately, accidents do happen. You can't predict them, but there are candidates. One of the most obvious is today's Hooveresque obsession with cutting the federal budget deficit. Almost every politician in Washington, from die-hard liberals to true-believer conservatives, now seems obsessed with the idea that budget surpluses are the key to long-term economic health and wealth. This almost religious belief that a balanced federal budget will be a panacea for our economy is echoed on Wall Street, which applauds every move by Washington to cut spending.

Deficit woes of countries like Argentina illustrate the disasters that can happen to countries that allow their debt to get too far out of control. The actual level of U.S. government debt, however, is only a very small part of the country's overall debt. In addition, the U.S. government's "safety net" has been a major factor softening the blow of declining living standards over the past twenty years. The very deficit spending that politicians are demonizing now has undeniably pumped billions into the economy, creating jobs and stimulating spending.

As of this writing, the annual federal government budget is about $170 billion in the red. Consequently, to balance it would require some combination of massive spending cuts and tax increases. Regardless of which option is chosen, the effect on the economy will be the same: a contractionary fiscal policy leading to slower economic growth.

Most dangerous would be if politicians succeed in passing a balanced budget amendment. Government would be locked in a straitjacket long after the current crop of officials is an historical footnote, just as it was to a degree under the gold standard. It would be unable to boost growth through spending and tax cuts in tough times, until the amendment was repealed.

In bad times, vigorous budget cutting or something more subtle but equally devastating—such as high tariffs—would be a complete disaster. In effect, it would compound the deflationary effect of a stock market meltdown, just as it did in the 1930s when balanced budget–obsessed President Herbert Hoover kept federal fiscal policy on a contractionary course. Like then, the result could be a wrenching depression from which the only release would be hyperinflation.

Call us crazy. But our belief is that government will hold to the lesson of 1929 in any future crisis. Ideologies such as deficit cutting tend to be evanescent in the face of political realities. But it's still possible that politicians could make a disastrous wrong move. Also, we could confront a situation over which the government does not have control—when investor selling and consumer panic would be so severe that the economy and financial markets collapse no matter what public officials do.

In the final analysis, a deflationary depression is unlikely to occur. And even should this calamity strike, the ultimate result is still likely to be rapid inflation, as the government attempts to dig the country out of the mess by pumping up money supply growth to third world levels.

Faster inflation is still the way to bet for the decade to come. The threat of deflation, however, can't be ruled out. That makes it not only worthwhile but absolutely essential to hold bonds in your portfolio.

Bonds That Beat Deflation

Bonds not only hold their ground during deflationary times, they actually prosper, even during full-blown depressions.

During the first part of the Great Depression from 1929–1932, for example, prices fell at an average annual rate of 6.4 percent. Stocks and precious metals lost more than 20 percent a year. Top-quality bonds, however, gained 5 percent annually. Coupled with the steep drop in the inflation rate, that added up to an average annual real return of 11.4 percent.

DEFLATION WINNERS AND LOSERS		
Assets	Nominal Return 7/29 to 4/33 (inf low)*	Nominal Return 7/29 to 6/32 (stk low)†
Stocks (S&P 500)	-23.67%	-44.12%
Small Stocks	-33.07	-53.13
Intermediate Bonds	4.99	4.40
Long-Term Bonds (Govt)	5.26	4.55
Long-Term Bonds (Corp)	5.04	2.97
Gold/Silver	-19.80	-19.80
Farmland	-12.30	-12.30
Cash (T-Bills)	1.75	2.28
CPI	-8.08	-7.80

*To low point in inflation
† To stockmarket low

Why do bonds prosper in times of deflation? Because the cash flow streams they pay are fixed. As money gains value relative to goods and services, those cash flow streams become ever more valuable. Also, real interest rates are typically very high because interest rates can't fall as fast as prices. That spells fat returns for bondholders. It also keeps economic growth slow, which keeps a lid on inflation—leading to further bond market gains.

Let's take an example similar to the one we used in chapter 9 to discuss real interest rates. Suppose you have $100,000 and inflation is falling 5 percent a year—in other words, deflation is running at a 5 percent annual rate. Your choices are to buy a $100,000 house or to buy a bond for the same amount that's yielding 7 percent. That's a real interest rate on the bond of 12 percent (7 percent yield plus 5 percent deflation rate).

If you buy the house, your investment will be worth $95,000 a year later, due to the 5 percent deflation rate. In contrast, if you buy the bond, you'll now have $107,000. Thanks to deflation, you'll be able to buy the same house and have $12,000 left over.

Clearly, during times of deflation, buying the bond is a better move than investing in a real asset like real estate. There is one caveat to this rule, however: The bond must be of the highest credit quality.

In times of deflation and depression, high debt levels are harder and harder to manage. The weaker the economy, the more financially weaker individuals, companies and even governments become prone to defaults.

Only those entities with the surest cash flow streams are assured of maintaining their interest payments to bondholders regardless of how bad things get. In a full-blown deflationary depression, that boils down to AAA-rated corporations and municipalities and the U.S. government.

With the power to tax, Uncle Sam can always raise money to finance himself and to pay off his bonds. No other government or company has that power. No matter how bad things get, it's virtually inconceivable that the U.S. government would go belly up. During the Great Depression of the 1930s, for example, Treasury bonds kept right on making their interest payments. And, should a future depression be set off by a budget-balancing federal policy, Treasurys would be even more secure.

As a result, U.S. Treasury paper is the only completely safe way to buy bonds for all environments. High-yield, low-quality "junk" bonds, including those mentioned in the last chapter, would be among the first to fall in a deflationary environment. So while junk bonds are good investments in inflationary times, only Treasurys would make suitable hedges against deflation.

Because deflation increases the future value of money, bonds with the longest maturities would enjoy the sharpest price increases; thirty-year Treasury bonds are the best example. And thirty-year "zero coupon bonds," which sell for a discount to their face value and pay no current interest, would probably do the best.

Over the really long pull, including all ranges of inflation, the best-performing bonds are intermediate-term securities, which generally mature in between five and ten years. Shorter maturities mean that these bonds will lose far less ground to inflation in coming years. Also, in mid-1995 their yields are rarely more than half a percentage point behind those of long-term paper. You can buy Treasurys at any brokerage, or you can use the Treasury Direct program, which allows you to buy bonds directly from the Treasury. Most banks have information on this program.

Bond mutual funds are another alternative. These let you own a large, diversified portfolio of bonds for a relatively low price. Many have done well in all kinds of markets, even while throwing off strong yields. Keep in mind, however, that fund managers often adjust their holdings. If a manager guesses wrong about the markets, your fund may perish rather than profit from deflation. Stick with funds that hold only top-quality securities like Treasurys. Low-expense funds like those in the Vanguard family are best.

Whichever option you choose for your "deflation insurance," you can sleep easier knowing that something in your portfolio will stand up against that worst of all worlds: economic depression. Just as with an auto or home insurance policy, you hopefully won't ever need it. But in an environment as volatile and uncertain as the next ten years are likely to be, it's nice to have bonds.

EPILOGUE

On September 6, 1996, as this book was being readied to go to press, a rather remarkable thing happened. The U.S. government announced the August unemployment rate had fallen to 5.1 percent, the lowest level of this decade. At the same time, hourly earnings rose at a huge annualized rate of about 6 percent.

These reports were just the latest in a series proclaiming the arrival of extremely rapid economic growth—the kind of news that usually has policymakers worried about controlling inflation. But what was the government's response to these clear warning signs? Don't worry, be happy.

The president's chief economic advisor, Joseph Stiglitz, hastened to assure Wall Street that there were no inflationary implications from the data. In fact, he asserted that the Federal Reserve Board "no longer needs to stamp out inflation before it happens." And he claimed, "If you do things cautiously with an economy that has been stable for a long time you have greater scope to do careful exploration."

This amazing bit of "wisdom," which no prominent economist came forward to challenge, had evidently been acquired at some point between 1994 and 1996. In 1994, a so-called stable economy was actually leaping friskily ahead. Then, however, the Fed acted aggressively to raise short-term interest rates to head inflation off at the pass. Wall Street clearly regarded this preventive strike as a stunning success.

The economy, which was growing at a better than 4 percent clip at the start of 1994, glided down to a more sustainable level of below 2 percent. Inflation had threatened to accelerate at the beginning of 1994. But it remained tame. In 1995, the economy continued along this slow-growth, low-inflation path.

In contrast, at least through mid-September 1996, the Fed has sat on its hands. If it really is basing its inaction on Mr. Stiglitz's maxim—i.e., lessons about the economy supposedly mastered since 1994—it's quite a feat. In fact, it's somewhat akin to a student managing to learn calculus between third and fourth grade without ever having been exposed to the subject. Not even Einstein or Newton could have done that.

More likely, the real lesson learned since 1994 is that even a modest amount of Fed tightening may be good news for stocks and bonds. But it's terrible news for incumbent politicians. Just ask some of the former Democratic congressmen and senators who got kicked out of office in 1994, in one of the major turnarounds in American politics. Or think back to 1992, when incumbent President George Bush received less than 40 percent of the vote.

The Fed's refusal to act, at least up to September 1996, is a clear acknowledgment that merely modest growth—the price of clamping down on inflation—is political suicide. And if higher inflation is the consequence of more rapid growth, so be it. In other words, by failing to raise interest rates, the Fed is conducting a very inflationary monetary policy.

The ultimate repercussions will be quite staggering. Inflation is much more a threat in late 1996 than in 1994. Most important are labor costs, which were tame in 1994 and are clearly accelerating in late 1996. At the same time, productivity—especially in the all-important service sector—continues to go nowhere.

The fact that few economists object to this Fed policy is a clear sign that inflation has passed from the front burner of economic concerns to the back. The hot issue today for both politicians and economists is growth. And that's likely to remain the case for the foreseeable future.

We're not completely cynical about the Fed. But regardless of their charter to be "independent," Fed governors must be appointed by politicians. And as we pointed out in chapter 1, politicians must answer to the deep-seated economic concerns of the American public in order to be reelected. With productivity stagnating, education's window of opportunity closing, commodity prices starting to rise and debt levels at record highs, Americans' concerns can only be quelled by very strong economic growth, and that always brings on accelerating inflation. The Fed has no other political choice than to inflate.

As we've pointed out in this book, however, there is also a compelling economic argument to pump up growth. Even in the rapidly growing economy of 1996, personal bankruptcies reached all-time highs. In fact, approximately 1 percent of all American households will probably declare bankruptcy in 1996. That's not surprising, considering there have been very few months during the economic expansion in which consumer debt did not rise at least twice as fast as consumer income.

Despite strong economic growth, the consumer has been growing ever weaker. And if the consumer's situation is going from bad to worse when the economy is on a roll, what will happen if things slow down? No one knows, including the Fed. The financiers of the massive consumer debt burden will certainly be hard-pressed. As a whole, the banking system has about three times its net worth lent out to the consumer, mainly in the form of personal loans and credit-card debt. Citicorp currently has over five times its net worth lent out. Slowing down growth under these circumstances is clearly playing with fire for consumers and banks alike.

The stock market is very much part of the uncertain and potentially disastrous equation of consumer incomes and debt. One measure of how important the stock market is to overall economic activity is the ratio of market valuation to overall GDP. Recently, many analysts have pointed out that the ratio of the value of all stocks to GDP is approaching an all-time record of 100 percent, even higher than in 1929.

A crash in the market would therefore wipe out an absolutely devastating amount of wealth. But even more worrisome is the fact that consumers' incomes over the past generation have not kept up with GDP growth. And this means the ratio of the stock market to incomes is in the stratosphere.

This ratio is so high that if the market corrected by 20 percent, it would be the equivalent of about a 35 percent drop in family income. No one knows the exact effect a real market correction would have on the economy. But clearly we would be in no man's land, with the potential for disastrous depressionary consequences.

Remember all the predictions of economic doom in 1987? The reason they missed the mark was that the decline in the market did not spread to the rest of the economy. Given the far higher level of participation in the stock market this time around, we would not be so lucky.

The bottom line: There is a political and economic necessity to inflate. As we pointed out in chapter 6, inflation probably reached a generational bottom in late 1993. As this book goes to press, 1996 is looking like it will be known as the year in which inflation began a long and sustained march upward.

The climb will be slow and probably unrecognizable to many in the early years, but it will be inexorable. Inflation's eventual peak will be many years down the road, and at levels much higher than those that prevail today. The best way to survive and thrive: Let the investment tenets outlined in this book be your guide.

INDEX